THE COMMONWEALTH AND INTERNATIONAL LIBRARY
Joint Chairmen of the Honorary Editorial Advisory Board
SIR ROBERT ROBINSON, O.M., F.R.S., LONDON
DEAN ATHELSTAN SPILHAUS, MINNESOTA
Publisher: ROBERT MAXWELL, M.C., M.P.

LIBRARY AND TECHNICAL INFORMATION DIVISION
General Editor: G. CHANDLER

A HISTORY OF CHILDREN'S READING AND LITERATURE

A HISTORY OF CHILDREN'S READING AND LITERATURE

BY

ALEC ELLIS

LECTURER IN LIBRARY WORK WITH YOUNG PEOPLE
SCHOOL OF LIBRARIANSHIP
LIVERPOOL COLLEGE OF COMMERCE

PERGAMON PRESS

OXFORD · LONDON · EDINBURGH · NEW YORK
TORONTO · SYDNEY · PARIS · BRAUNSCHWEIG

Pergamon Press Ltd., Headington Hill Hall, Oxford
4 & 5 Fitzroy Square, London W.1
Pergamon Press (Scotland) Ltd., 2 & 3 Teviot Place, Edinburgh 1
Pergamon Press Inc., 44–01 21st Street, Long Island City, New York 11101
Pergamon of Canada Ltd., 6 Adelaide Street East, Toronto, Ontario
Pergamon Press (Aust.) Pty. Ltd., Rushcutters Bay,
Sydney, New South Wales
Pergamon Press S.A.R.L., 24 rue des Écoles, Paris 5e
Vieweg & Sohn GmbH, Burgplatz 1, Braunschweig

Printed in Great Britain by A. Wheaton and Co. Ltd., Exeter

TO ANNE, MALCOLM, AND ALISON

Contents

List of Illustrations

ix

Preface

THE enfranchisement of the working people in urban areas in 1867 necessitated that they should be educated in order that they might exercise wisely their new privileges and responsibilities. Robert Lowe, a former Vice-President of the Committee of Council on Education and a man of limited vision where the education and enfranchisement of the masses were concerned, was among the first to recognize the need for the former on the realization of the latter. In a parliamentary speech after the passing of the Reform Bill in July 1867, he expressed his belief that "it will be absolutely necessary that you should prevail on our future masters to learn their letters". This statement has been popularized as "We must educate our masters", a phrase which may be considered to be the view of educationists to the present day.

In this book the development of working-class education in England and Wales has been traced through the 19th century to the present decade. The pattern of educational activity has been related to the methods undertaken in the schools, and the extent to which books have been used in the furtherance of literacy. It will be seen that not only has there been a lack of conviction on the part of numerous educationists as to the value of books in schools, but at various periods there has been positive opposition to their availability. At first there was antagonism to the use of secular literature, and later the exponents of scientific and technical education attempted to relegate books to a subsidiary position in the curriculum.

During the 19th century the school was the only possible source for the majority of children of good quality literature, although it was sometimes available in the form of prizes. If no books were provided at school, as was frequently the case, the children were deprived of reading material of any kind. Toward the close of the 19th century and throughout the 20th century, public libraries have been increasingly influential not only in the loan of books, but also in an advocacy of their intrinsic merit in the development of the individual.

My aim has been to describe some of the factors which were contributory or detrimental to the growth of literacy, including educational provision, the use of books in schools, the availability of school and public libraries, and the parallel evolution of recreational literature of all kinds. Prior to the last three decades, which have witnessed the development of paper-covered books, few children could have owned personal collections of any size.

The growth of literacy has been undermined by the use of such unsatisfactory instructional methods that large numbers of pupils have learned adequately neither the mechanics of reading nor their application to the understanding of different types of literature. In view of this the demand has been for trivial recreational writings in which the vocabulary and style are of a poor standard, and publishers have ensured their continued prosperity by making such literature available in large quantities. Many would complain that parents could do more to help their children, but they are in fact themselves representatives of a previously neglected generation. Parents who have not found or been led to discover an interest in reading, or have abandoned it in despair at their own ineptitude, surely cannot be expected to encourage their children in literary pursuits. In addition, there has been an apparent inability on the part of many teachers to recognize the value of books and, all too often, the library profession has been obsessed with techniques to the exclusion of all else, not least the reading needs of young people.

Social factors have often been the cause of a retarded growth in literacy. Poor environments have for generations resulted in physical and emotional disorders in children which have successively entailed absence from school and backwardness in the basic subjects of the curriculum. In the present work, references to the social and economic background of the working people have been made only in passing. For an informed view of that aspect the reader would be advised to refer to *The Common People* by G. D. H. Cole and Raymond Postgate.

I wish to thank Mr. A. S. Bishop, B.A., Senior Lecturer in Education, St. Katharine's College of Education, Liverpool, who has been kind enough to read the manuscript and to guide me through the complexities of educational history, particularly on the work of the Committee of Council on Education. I am also grateful to Mr. J. E. Vaughan, M.A., Tutor Librarian, the University of Liverpool, School of Education, who has read the manuscript and has given me the benefit of his experience in the bibliography of education. I should also like to thank the staff of the Picton Library, Liverpool, the staff of the Bootle Public Library, and Mr. John Williams, B.A., A.L.A., Librarian of St. Katharine's College, Liverpool, who have been so helpful to me in my search for relevant material. Finally, my work has been simplified once more by the willing co-operation of my wife, who has read, criticized, and frequently prevailed on me to improve upon parts of the manuscript. However, if faults exist the responsibility is, of course, mine alone.

I would claim to have uncovered a great deal of information which has been concealed for more than a century, and in so doing I hope to have made some small contribution to educational and literary history. The element of research has been secondary in importance to the amount of pleasure I have derived in writing this book, and if some of this is conveyed to the reader I shall be more than satisfied.

ALEC ELLIS

Childwall April 1967

CHAPTER 1

Light in the Darkness
1740–1830

DURING the 18th century the Industrial Revolution resulted in a movement of industry from the home to the factory, from hand to power, and from agriculture to the coalfield. The concentration of working people in the new industrial towns in the early 19th century made it imperative that, if they were not to threaten the security of the Establishment as in France, they must receive some form of education.

Educational activity was particularly manifest during the years of economic depression between 1814 and 1850. Economic factors resulted in a national state of social unrest which both Church and State came to recognize could be controlled only by the extension of education. In these years the Spa Fields riots of 1816 coincided with Brougham's *Enquiry into the Education of the Lower Orders of the Metropolis*, the Select Committee into *The State of Children in the Manufactures of the United Kingdom*, and Robert Owen's infants' school at New Lanark. The depression of 1819–20 and the Peterloo and other disturbances coincided with an *Enquiry into Charitable Funds* and a Parish School Bill. This correlation between education and economic and social tension was evident in all periods of depression throughout the 19th century, especially during the short-term cycles occurring within each of them.

Sunday schools had been a partial answer to the problem of education in the late 18th and early 19th centuries. They did not interfere with the weekday occupations in which children were engaged and so were not a burden on the financial resources of the poor. In 1785 a Society for the Establishment and Support of Sunday Schools was founded, and within a decade approximately 250,000 children were in attendance. When the Sunday School Union was founded in 1803 there were 7125 Sunday schools with 88,860 teachers and 844,728 pupils. At first both religious and secular instruction was provided, but as the movement grew paid teachers were replaced by volunteers and instruction became increasingly religious in character. As the demand for literacy continued to increase it became evident that the task was not one which could be adequately undertaken by Sunday schools, but that it was necessary to establish "a national system of Day schools".

The National Society for Promoting the Education of the Children of the Poor in the Principles of the Established Church was formed in 1811 with the intention that "the national religion of the country should be made the foundation of national education". In 1814 the British and Foreign School Society grew out of the earlier Lancasterian Society, and in this instance, while the Bible was to be introduced to children, it was to be presented "without note or comment, to the exclusion of the formularies of any particular Church".

Numerous books were available for educational purposes, many of which were written to interest their readers. Textbooks had been published for centuries in keeping with the changing trends in education. In the 18th century John Newbery issued *The Circle of the Sciences* (1745) in 7 volumes, which continued to be printed for more than 50 years. Another notable work was Richmal Mangnall's *Historical and Miscellaneous Questions* (1798), which was in use until after the Education Act of 1870. Early 19th-century examples were Darton & Harvey's *The Decoy of English Grammar* (1819) and Mrs. Ward's *Child's Guide to Knowledge*, the 2nd edition of which appeared in 1828.

Mrs. Marcet wrote simple books such as *Conversations on Chemistry* (1805), *Conversations on Natural Philosophy* (1819), and many others, all of which were very popular and were published in numerous editions.

Histories and geographies of England were fairly prolific but varied in quality and subject interest. The use in many of them of stilted dialogues was criticized by educationists. Outstanding histories included Mrs. Markham's *History of England* (1823) and Lady Calcott's *Little Arthur's History of England* (1835). Sir Richard Phillips, under the name of Rev. J. Goldsmith (one of his many pseudonyms), published *An Easy Grammar of Geography* (new edition, 1806) in which he included sections on the continents, the terrestrial and celestial globes, questions, exercises, and a lengthy gazetteer.

In addition to school books "children's books" were available at this time, published with the purpose of giving their readers pleasure, and not principally to teach them or to provide them with moral guidance. There were no children's books in England before 1600 (although there were numerous school books and guides to conduct), nor were they recognized as an identifiable branch of English literature until approximately 1750. It is, however, quite arbitrary to draw a distinction between "children's books" and "school books", and even after 1750 the difference was only partial.

In the years before a special literature for children appeared, young people adopted books and stories as their own. They read the romances of the Middle Ages, such as the tales of Robin Hood and Bevis of Southampton. John Bunyan's allegory *The Pilgrim's Progress* (1678) was very popular in adapted editions, as were Daniel Defoe's *Robinson Crusoe* (1719) and Jonathan Swift's socially satirical *Gulliver's Travels* (1726). Young people carefully ignored the morals and innuendoes with which these and similar books were filled, and extracted the delightful stories which have retained their favour for generations.

The availability of children's books was directly dependent upon the willingness of publishers to handle literature for the younger age group. John Newbery was the earliest publisher recognized for his association with children's books. In 1745 he established his business at the sign of "The Bible and Sun" in St. Paul's Churchyard, and at that address his successors were located for many years. Newbery used as his material the nursery lore of preceding generations and achieved his success in meeting the demands of the new urban middle classes which emerged as a

A Little Pretty
POCKET-BOOK,
Intended for the
INSTRUCTION and AMUSEMENT
OF
LITTLE MASTER *TOMMY*,
AND
PRETTY MISS *POLLY*.
With Two Letters from
JACK the GIANT-KILLER;
AS ALSO
A BALL and PINCUSHION;
The Use of which will infallibly make *Tommy*
a good Boy, and *Polly* a good Girl.

To which is added,
A LITTLE SONG-BOOK,
BEING
A *New Attempt* to teach Children the Use of
the *English Alphabet*, by Way of Diversion.

LONDON:
Printed for J. NEWBERY, at the *Bible and Sun*
in St. *Paul's Church-Yard.* 1767.
[Price Six-pence bound.]

FIG. 1.   Title page from John Newbery's *A Little Pretty Pocket Book*. 1767 edition.

consequence of the Industrial Revolution. John Harris managed Newbery's activities before he succeeded as head of the firm in 1821. This publishing house was responsible for the production of literature of a relatively entertaining character including the famous *A Little Pretty Pocket Book* (1744) (Fig. 1) and William Roscoe's *The Butterfly's Ball* (1807) (Fig. 2).

Newbery's did not maintain their supremacy in children's book publishing but were superseded by John Marshall of Aldermary Churchyard, who had on his list approximately 70 children's books between 1780 and 1790. Marshall was antagonistic to books of fantasy, and among his authors were Dorothy and Mary Jane Kilner and Lady Eleanor Fenn.

In the years between 1780 and 1800 an increasing number of publishers interested themselves in books for the young, among whom were Darton & Harvey; Stockdale of Piccadilly; Joseph Johnson; Dean & Munday; Vernon & Hood; Baldwin, Cradock & Joy; Taylor & Hessey; and Lackington. Longmans and Rivington also maintained departments which were concerned with children's books.

The prevalent view in the 18th century was that children's stories should always be designed to inculcate a moral: no sooner did the young begin to enjoy their reading than they were called upon to reflect. Initially, morals were appended to the stories as in the tales of Perrault and the fables of Aesop, but it became the practice to interweave them with the narrative. These stories were in the tradition of an earlier Puritan literature which had been written "with so strong a didactic and religious bias that to many they seem not to be children's books at all" (Darton). Outstanding examples of the moral tale were Thomas Day's *Sandford and Merton* (published by Stockdale, 1783/9) (Fig. 3), Mrs. Trimmer's *The History of the Robins* (published by Longmans, 1786) (Fig. 4), John Aikin and Anna Barbauld's *Evenings at Home* (1792/6), and Maria Edgeworth's *The Parent's Assistant* (published by Joseph Johnson, 1796). Many of the writers owed their inspiration to Jean Jacques Rousseau and, while the relationship between the moral tale and the earlier Puritan literature is manifest, the immediate influence was French.

A variation on the moral tale which appeared in the early years of the 19th century was the Sunday story, or religious fiction. The availability of healthy reading matter was negligible,

THE

BUTTERFLY'S BALL

AND THE

Grasshopper's Feast

BY MR. ROSCOE

To which is added

AN ORIGINAL POEM

ENTITLED

A Winter's Day

By MR. SMITH, of Stand

𝕷𝖔𝖓𝖉𝖔𝖓:

Printed for J. HARRIS, *successor to* E. NEWBERY,
*At the original Juvenile Library, corner
of St. Paul's Church-yard*

1807

FIG. 2.   Title page from William Roscoe's *The Butterfly's Ball.*
1807 edition.

THE

HISTORY

OF

SANDFORD & MERTON

A Work
intended for the ufe of Children.

BY THOMAS DAY, ESQ.

Suffer little children to come unto me,
and forbid them not.

EMBELLISHED WITH FRONTISPIECES.

The Tenth Edition Corrected.

IN THREE VOLUMES
VOL. I.

LONDON:
Printed for JOHN STOCKDALE, Piccadilly
1801.

FIG. 3.   Title page from Thomas Day's *The History of Sandford and Merton.* Vol. I. 1801 edition.

but the successful sales of Hannah More's *Cheap Repository* tracts showed that there was a potential market for inexpensive religious literature. Since 1699 the Society for the Promotion of Christian Knowledge had been a pioneer in the field, and in 1799 the London Missionary Society formulated plans for a similar organization. The resulting Religious Tract Society became aware that children were not entertained by the majority of its publications, and in 1805 inaugurated a new series which was to capture the hawkers' market and counteract "the profane and vicious tracts profusely circulated by them". R.T.S. literature included such titles as *The Fortune Teller's Conjuring Cap*, *The Wonderful Cure of General Naaman*, and *The Stingy Farmer's Daughter*. Mrs. Sherwood wrote tracts prolifically and among her more substantial publications were *Little Henry and His Bearer* (1814) and *The History of the Fairchild Family* (1818/47) (Fig. 5).

Moral tales continued to appear throughout the 19th century and frequently assumed an instructional purpose. This had been exemplified in the dialogues of *Sandford and Merton* and in the work of Maria Edgeworth. During the reign of George IV a large number of Questions, Catechisms, and Guides to Knowledge appeared. Representative works of the period included Maria Hack's *Winter Evenings; or, tales of travellers* (1818), *Grecian Stories* (1824), *Geological Sketches* (1831), Mary Elliott's *Rural Employments* (1820), and Rev. W. Bingley's *Useful Knowledge* (1825). These authors differed in the approach to their work but were in complete agreement as to the necessity for presenting knowledge. The characters in the stories used words of Latin origin rather than the homelier Anglo-Saxon, which would have rendered their converse less stilted and made them more sympathetic to their readers.

In these circumstances fairy tales received continual criticism, and "almost anyone conscious of a moral sense disliked them heartily" (Field). At the beginning of the 19th century the moral tale was dominant but was challenged effectively by Roscoe's *The Butterfly's Ball* (1807), Mrs. Dorset's *The Peacock at Home* (1807), Charles Lamb's *Prince Dorus* and *Tales from Shakespeare*

THE

HISTORY OF THE ROBINS

FOR THE INSTRUCTION OF CHILDREN ON THEIR
TREATMENT OF ANIMALS.

By MRS. TRIMMER.

WITH TWENTY-FOUR ILLUSTRATIONS FROM DRAWINGS BY

HARRISON WEIR.

LONDON
GRIFFITH AND FARRAN
SUCCESSORS TO NEWBERY AND HARRIS
THE CORNER OF ST. PAUL'S CHURCHYARD

FIG. 4.   Title page from Mrs. Trimmer's *The History of the Robins.*

(1807) for which he collaborated with his sister Mary. As early as 1818 Sir Richard Phillips published his volume of *Popular Fairy Tales* but with few exceptions the world of the supernatural was banished by the educationists.

The potential bookshelf of British children was greatly enriched by translations and other literary influences from Europe. Moral tales were influenced by Mme de Genlis and Arnaud Berquin in the later decades of the 18th century. Educational ideas were introduced into England by French emigrés after 1789, and there was also a reaction toward simplicity and virtue when publicity was given to the sensual excesses of the French court. French influence was present in the fairy tales of Charles Perrault, which were probably translated into English in 1729, and also in the 41 volume *Le Cabinet des Fées* (1785/9), which included Mme de Beaumont's *Beauty and the Beast*. French was the first European language into which *The Tales from the Arabian Nights* were translated (between 1704 and 1717), and shortly afterward this edition by Antoine Galland was translated into English and circulated in the chapbook market.

In 1823 editions began to appear of Edgar Taylor's translation of Grimm's *Popular German Stories*, and in the early years of the century Johann Wyss' *The Swiss Family Robinson*, from Switzerland, was published.

There was a regular traffic in books between England and the United States. In the 17th century *The New England Primer* was probably the first American book to be read by English children, and its contents were familiar to them for over a century. In the early years of the 19th century English editions were published of the instructional works of Samuel Goodrich (Peter Parley) and, to a lesser extent, Jacob Abbott, and of the entertaining works of Washington Irving and J. Fenimore Cooper. Copyright was not recognized between Britain and the United States until 1891, and literary piracy continued throughout the century.

Having surveyed the availability of recreational literature for children between 1740 and 1830, it is relevant to discuss the extent to which it was accessible to the audience for whom it was

THE HISTORY

OF THE

FAIRCHILD FAMILY;

OR,

𝕿𝖍𝖊 𝕮𝖍𝖎𝖑𝖉'𝖘 𝔐𝖆𝖓𝖚𝖆𝖑:

BEING A

COLLECTION OF STORIES

CALCULATED TO SHOW THE

IMPORTANCE AND EFFECTS OF A RELIGIOUS
EDUCATION.

BY

MRS. SHERWOOD,

AUTHOR OF "HENRY MILNER," "ORPHANS OF NORMANDY,"
"HEDGE OF THORNS," &c.

FIFTEENTH EDITION.

LONDON:

J. HATCHARD AND SON, 187, PICCADILLY.

1845

FIG. 5.   Title page from Mrs. Sherwood's *The History of the Fair-child Family*. 1845 edition.

written. The fundamental factor to be considered is the retail price of children's books during the period.

In the 18th and early 19th centuries chapbooks cost 1*d*., 2*d*., and 6*d*. Kendrew commenced his chapbook business in 1803 and enjoyed a prosperous trade in toy books for children, which he sold at ½*d*. and 1*d*. (Fig. 6). Chapbooks were the principal reading

FRONTISPIECE.

This man doth wander round the town
With fruit, both fresh and sweet,
For those, who do attend their book,
And go both clean and neat.

THE

SILVER PENNY,

FOR THE

AMUSEMENT

AND

INSTRUCTION

OF

GOOD CHILDREN.

YORK:

Printed by J. Kendrew, Colliergate.

FIG. 6.   Frontispiece and title page from a chapbook published by Kendrew of York.

matter of the working people until the early years of Victoria's reign, when they were superseded by penny fiction published by Lloyd & Reynolds and other unscrupulous publishers. Reward books were sold in bundles at prices which ranged from ½*d*. to 3*d*. for single copies, while large quantities could be purchased at 12*s*. per 100.

New books for adults in the first quarter of the 19th century were more expensive than before, and novels in their usual size

(12mo) were 5*s*. or 6*s*. This was due partly to the lack of enterprise endemic in British publishing, to the higher wages earned by compositors, and to the high cost of materials.

In contrast, the children's publications of Darton, Dean & Munday and of Marshall were normally sold at either 6*d*. or 1*s*. Similar prices to those for adult works were, however, paid for Godwin's publications, among which were Lamb's *Tales From Shakespeare* (2 volumes), which in 1809 cost 8*s*., and *Mrs. Leicester's School* at 3*s*. 6*d*.

The catalogue issued by the R.T.S. in 1820 listed children's books in "neat, stiff covers", including *The Pilgrim's Progress* at 8*d*. to members of the Society and 10*d*. to other purchasers.

Between 1825 and 1830 cheaper books for adults became available due to the introduction of cloth-binding as a substitute for leather, but the majority of working people were still unable to afford them. Standard literature was available to the lower classes in the form of reward books, which probably came into existence almost as soon as the Sunday schools.

Whatever the glories of the Augustan age, the spirit of which pervaded 18th-century thought, it remains true that the mass of the people was illiterate and, as such, steeped in ignorance. On the threshold of a new century the first unsteady steps taken to provide education can be discerned in the work of the Sunday schools and educational societies. From 1750 a literature for children developed, the content of which was beyond the comprehension of the working people, but which was to evolve and play an increasingly important part in the growth of literacy as young people were able to read it. At first, children's books were directed at the middle classes, but increasingly in the 19th century the needs of the poorer majority were to be satisfied.

CHAPTER 2

The Dawn of Literacy
1830–1850

In 1833 the House of Commons voted a sum of £20,000 "for the purposes of education", an action which attracted very little attention at the time. The British and National Societies shared the grant and used it in the building of schools. The Educational Committee of the Wesleyan Conference was elected in 1837 to superintend all day, evening, and Sunday schools associated with that body; and the Catholic Institute of 1845 was superseded in 1847 by the Catholic Poor School Committee. Schools belonging to these organizations received the grants from the Government on conforming to the Management Clauses of 1846.

In 1839 a Committee of Council on Education was appointed by Order in Council "to superintend the application of any sums voted by Parliament for the purpose of promoting public education". Engels commented in 1844 that a mere £40,000 was devoted to public education in a budget of £55 million.

Provision for education was not made by the religious societies alone. The Factory Act of 1833 was the first legislation which represented a determined attempt to protect children in the textile industry; at the conclusion of their 8 hours of work, those between 9 and 13 were to attend schools provided by the employers. The Factory Act of 1844 obliged children between 8 and 13 to spend each week either three whole days or six half-days at school. In this way the system of "half-time" education commenced, which was not finally abandoned until 1922. In 1844 the hours of work were limited to $6\frac{1}{2}$ per day, either prior to or after the dinner hour, and in the former situation at least it is difficult to understand how children could derive any profit from the instruction they received.

The Poor Law Reform Act of 1834 stipulated that children in workhouses should receive 3 hours' instruction each day. However, in all the large towns children of the very poor did not attend school of any kind, either because they did not possess suitable clothes or because they were not provided with meals at regular times. The Ragged School Union was founded in 1844 "to promote the education of the waifs and strays of great cities", and while the instruction was rudimentary it was also gratuitous.

Sunday schools continued to provide facilities, but the instruction received in them was frequently limited by a deficiency of books, maps, and other apparatus. This was regrettable in that a large number of children obtained their only education from these schools.

Evening schools were available to serve the needs of children who were at work during the day. During the 1840's there was a considerable increase in the number of these schools which were generally attended by young people and adults of 13 years and upwards. They usually received instruction in the three R's between the hours of 7 or 8 p.m. and 9 or 10 p.m. from the master of the local national school. Frequently the sexes were segregated "so that no mischievous consequences may arise".

In 1839, 71% of the children in the South Wales mining area between 3 and 12 were not at school. The average length of school life on a national level rose from approximately 1 year in 1835 to 2 years in 1851. During the decade following the distribution to the religious societies of the first parliamentary grant, the standard of literacy remained low. The situation in the north-west was perhaps typical of the national level, in that a fair proportion of working-class children read with fluency but very few demonstrated by their expression that they understood what they read.

A report from the Midlands in 1844 revealed that of 11,782 children in attendance at elementary schools, 2449 boys and 1502 girls could read easy narratives but were unable to read the

Bible, whilst 1200 boys and 826 girls could read the Bible. 5805 children were familiar only with letters and monosyllables. Factory owners claimed that the majority of children employed by them had been taught to read, but reports of the Children's Employment Commission in 1842 showed that this claim was made of any child who knew his alphabet. In the 1840's more than 50% of the children aged 5 to 15 in Birmingham were not at school, a fact which increases the significance of the statistics of literacy in the Midlands at that time.

In the British Society's schools in 1846 only 10% of the boys could read with ease, and only $\frac{1}{2}$% with expression. The girls, however, showed greater proficiency, 5% being able to read with apparent understanding and 80% with ease. These standards were comparable with those which generally obtained in national schools.

The standards, however, were not uniformly poor throughout the country. An inspector of Midlands schools in 1844 submitted a report in 1847 for the southern counties of Berkshire, Hampshire, and Wiltshire. He found that a larger proportion of children could read in the south, and that of a population of 6213, 17% could read the Bible fluently, 50% could read simple passages from the Gospels, whilst the remaining 33% were learning letters and monosyllables.

It was the normal practice where books were provided in schools for the Bible to be used as the textbook for instruction in reading, a feature which was continuously criticized by inspectors after 1839. In the diocese of Winchester the schools were simply extensions of Sunday schools, and an adequate education for working-class children was thought to comprise an ability to recite the Church catechism and to master the mechanics of reading from the Bible. Children memorized the contents of the Bible so that it was impossible to test their reading ability unless they were presented with the same words in a different context. In 69 Midlands schools out of 103 for which returns were compiled in 1844, Bibles or extracts therefrom were the only form of reading

THE

JUVENILE READER;

CONSISTING OF

RELIGIOUS, MORAL, AND INTELLECTUAL INSTRUCTION;

EXERCISES IN

SPELLING, EXPLANATION, AND DERIVATION;

AND

AN APPENDIX,

CONTAINING

SELECT PIECES FOR RECITATION;

THE PRINCIPAL

PREFIXES, AFFIXES, AND ROOTS OF THE ENGLISH LANGUAGE,

WITH THEIR

LITERAL SIGNIFICATIONS, DERIVATIVES, AND COMPOUNDS.

BY N. LEITCH, F.E.I.S.

Author of "A History of Scotland," "The Instructive Reader,"
"The Monitorial Class Books," "The Young Scholar's Spelling Book,"
"A Brief Analysis of the Assembly's Shorter Catechism,"
"The Beginner's Scripture Catechism," "Exercises on the Map of Scotland," etc.

ONE HUNDRED AND TWENTIETH THOUSAND.

GLASGOW:

JOHN BURNET, WILLIAM COLLINS,

F. ORR & SONS, JAMES LUMSDEN & SON, D. CHAMBERS, G. & J. CAMERON:
OLIVER & BOYD, AND JOHNSTONE & HUNTER, EDINBURGH: JOHN
HEYWOOD, MANCHESTER: AND WILLIAM COLLINS, LONDON.

Price One Shilling and Sixpence.   Entered at Stationers' Hall.

FIG. 7.   Title page from Leitch's *The Juvenile Reader*. 1839.

material, but in most schools throughout England and Wales no attempt was made to provide books of any kind.

The house of Collins had issued its first school book in 1821 on commercial arithmetic, followed by a book of elocution. Collins attained success in 1836 when he published Leitch's *Practical and Economical Readers*, and in 15 years sold 1½ million copies. Leitch's *The Juvenile Reader* (1839) (Fig. 7) cost 1s. 6d., and the intention of the compiler was "to make such a selection as will serve to please, instruct, and profit the young". He was careful only to include material which would illustrate the perfections of the Divine Being, and to promote the temporal and eternal welfare of those into whose hands the compilation may be placed. The book contained extracts from religious writings, descriptions of objects, scientific articles, and poetry.

Among the publishers who produced books for elementary school children in the 1840's were the British and Foreign School Society, the Irish Commissioners of Education, the Edinburgh Sessional School, Messrs. Chambers, and the S.P.C.K. In 1844 the latter body issued its first *Educational Series* and selections from Lady Eleanor Fenn's series of graded reading primers, *Cobwebs to Catch Flies* (1783?). Kay-Shuttleworth compiled *The First Phonic Reading Book* (1843), which was approved by the Committee of Council on Education, but was subjected to scathing criticism in *The Quarterly Review*.

There was a shortage of suitable books, and this was only one of the difficulties which had to be overcome before the level of literacy could be raised. Very few books, if any, were compiled with specific attention to the educational needs of the working classes, and where they were available, they were not provided in sufficient quantities to supply the requirements of entire schools.

Quite apart from the lack of variety in books, many schools were unable to obtain them owing to poor financial circumstances. The salaries of teachers absorbed at least 75% of school income, whilst according to one inspector, books accounted for as little as 5 or 10% of the total expenditure. Teachers were inadequately remunerated so that in many cases all money which could be saved from school expenses was considered to be their due, and clergymen were often unable to provide adequate facilities for their schools from their own stipends.

A further difficulty was the price of secular books in relation to that for Bibles and Testaments. In 1844, a well bound and printed New Testament could be obtained from the S.P.C.K. for 6*d.*, whilst its 4th Reader cost 1*s.* 6*d.* The rules of the Society forbade the allowance of discounts on secular books, but they were available for Bibles and other books of a religious character. As long as this situation persisted it was unlikely that secular books would be introduced into schools in large numbers.

In spite of the general deficiency of books, a minority of schools contained them in quantities adequate to their needs. The school at Little Rissington in Gloucestershire was well supplied, whilst at Cheadle in Cheshire, there was a wide selection of entertaining and instructive tracts in use as Readers, which had been obtained from the S.P.C.K. The selections of books in schools in the eastern counties and the metropolitan area were said to have undergone great improvement during the mid-1840's.

Children were often required to provide their own books, which as a contribution to their education was negligible, for the books frequently bore no relationship whatever to the reading ability, intelligence, or maturity of the pupils. Books provided by parents were frequently "mere fragments, consisting of a few soiled leaves". (Committee of Council: Minutes, 1839/40.)

The availability of books in elementary schools in England and Wales compared unfavourably with Scotland and various European countries. An inspector referred to the practice of Scottish children carrying satchels of books to their homes at the end of a school day, where they could review the lessons they had already studied, or prepare for forthcoming work.

It was evident that the educational societies, managers of schools, and teachers were incapable of making the necessary provision of books and that substantial assistance must be forthcoming from an outside source. The inspectors appointed in 1839 were expected to inquire into the funds at the disposal of schools for books, and as a result of their findings, they recommended that grants should be made by the Committee of Council, as a means of ensuring the liberal distribution of books in schools. However, in a letter to inspectors in 1844 their lordships did "not feel themselves at liberty to make any grants for books".

Inspectors also advanced ideas on the suitability of content in books. One sought to introduce interesting books of moral teaching in the form of allegories and anecdotes. He considered that histories should illustrate life and manners, and instanced the work of Mrs. Markham. Also he recommended the use of suitably adapted biographies such as Plutarch's *Lives*, to encourage the possible emulation of heroes, or extracts from Camden's *Britannia*, Fuller's *Worthies*, and Drayton's *Polyolbion*.

A variety of opinions were voiced but they were not always related to the low standards of reading in elementary schools. Managers and teachers urgently required guidance as to the books which should be adopted for their pupils, and some recommended the publication of a list of books in addition to adequate financial assistance in their purchase.

Particular difficulty was encountered in Wales as regards its educational development. The industrialization of South Wales in the early years of the 19th century took place more rapidly than the equivalent urbanization in England, and resulted in a large concentrated population which did not speak English. Unfortunately the Government at Westminster refused to recognize the unique Welsh culture and attempted to replace it by English language and literature. In 1846 a Welsh Education Commission was appointed and it was discovered that the supply of books was quite inadequate and exclusively English. It was not for many years that the Government abandoned its attempt to anglicize the Welsh, and allowed the native language to assume its rightful place in the school curriculum.

In 1847 the Committee of Council agreed to reverse its decision regarding grants for books in schools, and resolved that it was expedient to encourage the introduction of "the most approved lesson books". Schedules of these books were prepared for the approbation of the Committee, and all books, for the purchase of which grants were made, were to be selected by school managers from the Schedules (Figs. 8–14).

Grants were made at a rate not exceeding 2s. for every pupil normally in attendance on condition that $66\frac{2}{3}\%$ of the value was subscribed by the schools. With reference to the proposed grants Kay-Shuttleworth informed the Vicar of King's Somborne in August 1848 that books would be obtainable by managers at $66\frac{2}{3}\%$ of the published price, but the official schedules defined the discount facilities as from 32% to 55%.

Two schedules were prepared in 1848, one of books and maps for the use of scholars and the other for teachers and pupil-teachers. It was intended to amend the Schedules, as particular books either ceased to be used or were introduced into schools. The publishing house of Longmans was appointed as agent of the Committee for the distribution of books to schools, and it was agreed that local managers should defray postal costs. Listed in the Schedules for the use of pupils were 83 books, 43 of which were reading books. Very few of the books had a retail price in excess of 2s. 6d., and almost 50 of the 83 cost less than 1s. The liberal discounts which were available rendered the prices even more attractive. In compiling the list the Committee of Council used as its basis works submitted by educational publishers and societies. The prerogative of rejection was exercised on two groups:

(1). the unsuitability of a work for elementary education; and
(2). the book belonging to a category of literature too numerous to be contained in a list.

The principal classes excluded from the list were ancient history, ancient and modern languages, biography, historical and geographical accounts of individual countries outside the British Isles; reading lesson books not forming part of a series; and collections of vocal music unaccompanied by instruction.

The schools of the National and British Societies were not the sole beneficiaries of the new grants as they had been in 1833.

SCHEDULE I.—LESSON BOOKS FOR THE SCHOLARS.

Reading Lesson Books. Educational Books—			Size of Paper on which it is printed.	No. of Sheets in Book.	No. of Pages in Book.	Size of Type in which it is printed.	No. and Size of Maps or Plates, if any.	No. of Woodcuts printed in same Pages with Type.	Description of Binding.	Price per Copy at which it is sold Retail to the Public. (s. d.)	Price per Copy at which it is offered to the Committee of Council on Education. (s. d.)
	Society for Promoting Christian Knowledge.	These books are in use chiefly in Church of England Schools connected with the National Society.									
The First Book			Double pott	1½	48	Pica	...	12	Printed wrapper	0 2	0 1½
The Second Book			Ditto	5	160	Small pica	...	13	Cloth limp	0 8	0 5¼
The Third Book			Demy	8	192	Ditto	...	...	Sheep	1 4	0 10
Reading Series—											
No. 1	Ditto.		Ditto	1⅔	60	Pica	...	...	Cloth limp	0 3	0 2
No. 2			Ditto	1	36	Long primer	...	...	Ditto	0 1½	0 1½
Moral and Intellectual Series—	Compiled by some of the chief officers of the British and Foreign School Society.	These books are in general use in schools of the British and Foreign School Society.									
No. 1, Daily Lesson Book.			Ditto	1	46	Various	None	3	Union	0 3	0 1½
No. 2 ditto.			Extra size equal to demy.	3½	120	Ditto	1	None	Ditto	1 0	0 7½
No. 3 ditto.			Royal	5½	192	Ditto	None	Ditto	Ditto	1 6	0 11
No. 4 ditto.			Ditto	9	324	Ditto	Ditto	.. 23	Ditto	2 0	1 0
Sequel to No. 1, in Sheets,			Demy	15	30	Ditto	Ditto	None	Folio sheets	3 0	1 9½
Sequel to ditto, No. 2											
The Reading Lesson Books—	Compiled and published under the authority of the Commissioners of National Education in Ireland.	These Reading Lesson Books were compiled for the National School established under the Board of Education in Ireland, but they are also extensively in use among all classes of schools in England, Wales, and Scotland.	Extra size equal to demy.	3¾	128	Long primer and brevier.	Ditto	Ditto	Union	0 8	0 5

FIGS. 8–14. Schedule of Lesson Books for the Scholars. (Reproduced from the Minutes of the Committee of Council on Education. Vol. I. 1847/48.)

The First	. .	. .	Printing demy	1	36	Pica	Ditto	Ditto	Printed wrapper	0 2	0 1
The Second	. .	. .	Ditto	5	178	Small pica	Ditto	Ditto	Cloth	0 7	0 4
The Third	. .	. .	Ditto	12	288	Ditto	Ditto	Ditto	Ditto	1 2	0 8
The Fourth	. .	. .	Ditto	15	358	Ditto	Ditto	Ditto	Ditto	1 4	0 9
The Fifth	. .	. .	Ditto	17½	420	Long primer	Ditto	76	Ditto	1 8	0 11
Sequel to Second	. .	. .	Ditto	6½	232	Small pica	Ditto	14	Ditto	0 9	0 5
Supplement to Fourth	. .	. .	Ditto	18½	444	Ditto	Ditto	None	Ditto	1 8	0 11
Reading Book for the use of Female Schools	. .	. .	Ditto	17½	420	Long primer	Ditto	Ditto	Ditto	1 8	0 10
First Reading Book	By the Rev. J. M. M'Culloch, LL.D.	Dr. M'Culloch's Series of Reading Lessons is in very general use in efficient middle-class schools, and the best Parochial and other Elementary Schools, in the north of England and Scotland. As their character has become known in the midland and southern counties of England, they have had a constantly increasing sale.	L. demy and third	½	24	Pica and minion	Ditto	Ditto	Printed wrapper	0 1¼	0 0¾
Second ditto	Ditto	Ditto	Ditto	1	48	S. pica & bourg.	Ditto	Ditto	Ditto	0 3	0 1¼
Third ditto	Ditto	Ditto	Ditto	3	144	Various	Ditto	Ditto	Sprinkled sheep	0 10	0 5¼
Series of Lessons in Prose and Verse	Ditto	Ditto	Demy and third	7 5/16	234	Ditto	Ditto	Ditto	Ditto	2 0	0 11¼
Course of Elementary Reading	Ditto	Ditto	Ditto	11¾	376	Ditto	Ditto	40	Coloured sheep, lettered.	3 0	1 5¾
Rural Spelling Book	By C. W. Johnson, F.R.S.	. .	Demy 12mo.	7	166	Ditto	. .	38	Embossed cloth, lettered.	1 6	0 8
The New Series of School Books—	Compiled for the Scottish School-Book Association.	This new series has been compiled under the superintendence of the chief members of the Scottish Schoolmasters' Association, and may be regarded as the work of the most intelligent members of that body. The use of these books is becoming more general in the parochial and private schools of Scotland.									

SCHEDULE I.—Lesson Books for the Scholars—*continued.*

			Size of Paper on which it is printed.	No. of Sheets in Book.	No. of Pages in Book.	Size of Type in which it is printed.	No. and Size of separate Maps or Plates, if any.	No. of Woodcuts printed in same Pages with Type	Description of Binding.	Price per Copy at which it is sold Retail to the Public.	Price per Copy at which it is offered to the Committee of Council on Education.
Reading Lesson Books—continued.										s. d.	s. d.
The Child's First Book	. .	. .	Double pott . .	¼	12	Double pica, &c.	. .	. .	Stitched . . .	0 1	0 0¼
No. 1, Primer . .	. .	. .	Demy and third .	¼	12	Small pica, &c.	. .	. .	Printed wrapper	0 1½	0 0¾
No. 2, Second Lessons	. .	. .	Demy	1	36	Long primer, &c.	. .	. .	Ditto . .	0 3	0 1½
No. 3, Third ditto .	. .	. .	Demy and third .	2¼	108	Ditto . .	. .	. .	½ bound flush, printed cover.	0 6	0 3
Manual of English Pronunciation, or Sequel to Third Lessons	. .	. .	Ditto . .	1	48	Ditto . .	. .	. .	Printed wrapper	0 4	0 2
Sheet Lessons . .	. .	. .	Extra double fcap.	15	30	Dble English, &c.	. .	. .	Not bound . .	3 0	1 5
No. 4, Readings in Prose and Verse	. .	. .	Demy and third .	3	144	Small pica, &c.	. .	. .	Cloth sd. on tape	0 10	0 5
No. 5, First Collection of Instructive Extracts	. .	. .	Extra double fcap.	7½	240	L. prim. & min.	. .	. .	Ditto . .	1 6	0 9
No. 6, Second Collection of Instructive Extracts	. .	. .	Ditto . . .	9¾	312	Ditto & minion	. .	. .	Ditto . .	2 0	1 0½
Reprints of Vocabularies from Nos. 5 and 6	. .	. .	Ditto . . .	1¼ & 4 pp.	52	Bourgeois . .	. .	. .	Printed wrapper	0 6	0 3
No. 1, Lessons for Schools	By the late Rev. A. Thomson, D.D.	Compiled by the late Rev. Dr. Andrew Thomson, of Edinburgh, an eminent divine of the Scottish Church. The circulation of these books is nearly confined to the Sessional Schools of Scotland.	Demy	1	30	Small pica . .	. .	. .	Ditto . .	0 3	0 1½
No. 2, ditto . .	Ditto . . .	Ditto	Demy and third .	3	144	Ditto . .	. .	. .	Cloth sd. on tape	0 10	0 5
No. 3, ditto . .	Ditto . . .	Ditto	Ditto . . .	3	144	Long primer .	. .	. .	Ditto . .	0 10	0 5
No. 4, ditto . .	Ditto . . .	Ditto	Ditto . . .	5	240	Ditto . .	. .	. .	Ditto . .	1 3	0 7½

The Juvenile Reader	By Neil Leitch .	A Reading Lesson Book for the first or second class of an elementary school used in Scotland.	Extra double fcap.	6¼	216	Ditto . .	. .	15	Coloured sheep, and titled.	1 6	0 9
Reading Disentangled; being a Series of Elementary Reading Lessons on Sheets	By the Author of "Peep of Day."	In very general use for the instruction of very young children in reading in all classes of Elementary Schools.	Foolscap broadside	37	37	Various . . .	. .	168	In sheets . . Japanned frame Mill board . .	6 0 12 0 12 0	4 0 7 0 7 6
Grammar and Etymology.											
Manual of English Grammar	By Rev. J. M. M'Culloch, LL.D.	A Grammar for an Elementary School of the highest class, but not adapted to an humble School. A proper Manual for Pupil-Teachers and for Teachers.	Demy and third .	3⅔	180	Ditto . .	None .	None .	Sprinkled sheep	1 6	0 6¼
An English Grammar for the use of Schools	By the Commissioners of National Education in Ireland.	. .	Printing demy . .	5	178	Brevier . . .	Ditto .	Ditto . .	Cloth . . .	0 8	0 4
Rudiments of English Grammar	By A. Reid, A.M. .	Extensively used by the Scholars of Elementary Schools in Scotland.	L. demy and third	$\frac{23}{24}$	46	Various . . .	Ditto .	Ditto .	Cloth limp . .	0 6	0 2
An Attempt to Simplify English Grammar	By Professor R. Sullivan.	Suitable for the Scholars of Elementary Schools.	Printing demy .	5 18mo	180	Brev. & nonpl.	. .	. .	Coloured cloth, stamped & letrd,	1 0	0 6
A System of English Grammar	By C. W. Connon .	Ditto	Crown and third .	5¼	168	Bourg. & minion	None .	None .	Cloth, lettered	2 6	1 2¼
An English Grammar .	By Allen and Cornwell.	Ditto	Demy 18mo. . .	4½	162	L. prim. & brev.	. .	. . .	Cloth	1 9	1 0¼
Grammar for Beginners	By Dr. Cornwell .	Ditto	Ditto . . .	2	72	Ditto . .	. .	. .	Ditto . .	1 0	0 7
An Initiatory Grammar of the English Language	By J. Millen . . .	Ditto	Demy and third .	2⅝	126	Bourg. & brev.	None	None .	Sprinkled sheep	1 0	0 5¾
An Elementary Etymological Manual	By W. Ross . . .	Ditto	Demy 18mo. .	1½	54	Principally Brev.	. .	. .	Stitched . .	0 6	0 3¼
Principles of English Grammar	No. 8 of the Scottish School Book Associations.	. .	Demy and third .	2½ & 8 pp.	128	Lg. primer, &c.	. . .	. .	Cloth sd. on tape	0 9	0 4¼
The Young Child's Grammar	Ditto . . .	. .	Demy	1	36	Bourgeois, &c. .	. .	. .	Printed wrapper	0 3	0 1¼
Outlines of Etymology.	By Rev. A. Wilson .	Suitable for the Scholars of Elementary Schools. Published by the Society for Promoting Christian Knowledge.	Ditto . . .	⅔	24	Long primer .	. .	. .	Paper wrapper .	0 1½	0 1

SCHEDULE I.—Lesson Books for the Scholars—*continued.*

			Size of Paper on which it is printed.	No. of Sheets in Book.	No. of Pages in Book.	Size of Type in which it is printed.	No. and Size of separate Maps or Plates, if any.	No. of Woodcuts printed in same Pages with Type.	Description of Binding.	Price per Copy at which it is sold retail to the Public.	Price per Copy at which it is offered to the Committee of Council on Education.
										s. d.	s. d.
Grammar and Etymology.—continued.											
The Pupil's Guide to English Etymology	By G. Manson	Suitable for the scholars of elementary schools.	Demy	3¾	132	Brevier	.	.	Half-bound, printed cover.	1 0	0 6
Arithmetic.											
The Intellectual Calculator	By J. T. Crossley and W. Martin.	These authors have long been among the most useful Officers of the British and Foreign School Society, and the book is generally adopted both in British and in other Schools.	Ditto	4	146	Various	1	None	Red sheep	1 8	1 0
First Book of Arithmetic	By the Commissioners of National Education in Ireland.	.	Printing demy	4¼	148	Brevier	None	None	Cloth	0 8	0 4
A Treatise on Arithmetic Elements of Book-keeping	Ditto / Ditto	. .	Ditto / Ditto	17 / ·5¼	408 / 126	Long primer / Ditto	Ditto / Ditto	Ditto / Ditto	Ditto / Ditto	2 6 / 0 10	0 11 / 0 5
A Treatise on the First Principles of Arithmetic	By Thomas Tate, Mathematical Master in the Battersea Training School.	A work of merit, containing a simple method of rendering both the principles and the practice of Arithmetic familiar to the Scholars of Elementary Schools.	Demy 12mo.	5	120	Ditto	.	.	Ditto	1 6	0 10¾
Exercises in Arithmetic for Elementary Schools	Ditto	Exercises to accompany the Tables, and adapted to the method, of Pestalozzi.	Ditto	7 & 4 pp.	179	Brevier [	.	.	Ditto	1 6	1 0
Arithmetical Questions	By W. M'Leod, lately Master of the Battersea Village School, and now of the Military Model School, Chelsea.	Well-selected Exercises on the same method.									

Title	Author	Remarks			Pages	Type			Binding		
Part 1			Ditto	3¾	88	Long primer			Stitched	1 0	0 7
Part 2			Ditto	3	72	Ditto			Ditto	1 0	0 7
Lessons on Arithmetic for Junior Classes	By James Trotter	Extensively in use in parochial Schools in Scotland.	L. demy and third	1	48	Various	None	None	Printed wrapper	0 6	0 1¼
Concise System of Practical Arithmetic	Melrose's, revised by A. Ingram and J. Trotter.	Extensively used in Parochial Schools and in Middle Schools in Scotland.	Demy and third	4 5⁄12	212	Ditto	None	None	Sprinkled sheep	1 6	0 7½
System of Practical Arithmetic	No. 11 of the Scottish School-Book Association.		Ditto	2¼	108	Bourgeois, &c.			Cloth sd. on tape	0 9	0 4½
Key to ditto	Ditto		Demy board	··	1	Brevier			Not bound	0 2	0 0¾
First Lessons in Practical Arithmetic	Ditto		Demy	1	36	Long Primer			Printed wrapper	0 3	0 1¼
Key to ditto	Ditto		Demy board	··	1	Bourgeois			Not bound	0 2	0 0¾
Geography.											
Geography Generalized	By Professor Sullivan	A book which should be read in all Elementary Schools in connection with the study of the Maps.	Foolscap	18 shts. 8vo	288	Bourg. and brev.	1 fcp. 4to	27	Coloured cloth, stamped and lettered.	2 0	1 3
A School Geography	By Dr. Cornwell	Written by a Master of the Normal School of the British and Foreign School Society in the Borough Road, and extensively used in British and other Schools.	Royal	9	318	Various			Cloth	3 6	2 1
Compendium of Geography	By the Commissioners of National Education in Ireland.		Printing demy	5½	196	Brevier	None	None	Ditto	1 0	0 5
An Introduction to Geography and History	By Professor Sullivan		Demy	4 18mo	144	Bourg. & minion	1 fcp. 4to	18	Coloured cloth, stamped and lettered.	1 0	0 6
Rudiments of Modern Geography	By A. Reid, A.M.	The first three very brief; for use with Maps.	L. demy and third	2½	120	Various	1½ in. in. 13×7¾	3	Sprinkled sheep	1 0	0 5¼
Outlines of Sacred Geography	Ditto		Ditto	1	48	S. pica and bourg.	None	1	Printed wrapper	0 6	0 1¼

SCHEDULE I.—Lesson Books for the Scholars—*continued*.

	By		Size of Paper on which it is printed.	No. of Sheets in Book.	No. of Pages in Book.	Size of Type in which it is printed.	No. and Size of separate Maps, or Plates, if any.	No. of Woodcuts printed in same Pages with Type	Description of Binding.	Price Per Copy at which it is sold retail to the Public. s. d.	Price per Copy at which it is offered to the Committee of Council on Education. s. d.
Geography—continued. The Young Child's Geography	No. 9 of the Scottish School-Book Association.		Demy	1	30	Long primer	.	.	Printed Wrapper	0 3	0 1½
Outlines of Modern Geography	No. 10, ditto		Extra double fcp.	3¾	120	S. pica & minion	.	.	¼ bound, flush, paper sides.	1 0	0 6
Geography of Palestine	By W. M'Leod, lately Master of the Battersea Village School, and now Master of the Military Model School, Chelsea.	The author has been successively the master of the Norwood School of Industry, of the Battersea Village School, and of the Military Model School, Royal Hospital, Chelsea.	Demy 12mo.	5	120	Long primer	1 demy 12mo.	.	Cloth	1 6	0 10¾
English History. A plain and short History of England	By the Bishop of Peterborough.		Demy	7¼	262	Long primer	1	.	Half-bound in Roan, lettered.	2 6	1 6
A School History of England	J. W. Parker		Demy 12mo.	27	648	Bourgeois	.	1	Blue Sheep	6 0	3 3
Mensuration. A Treatise on Mensuration	By the Commissioners of National Education in Ireland.		Printing demy	11¼	276	Long primer	None	174 Diagrams.	Cloth	1 6	0 8
Vocal Music. Wilhelm's Method of Teaching Singing adapted to English Use	By John Hullah	An excellent Manual, which has had a most extensive circulation.	Royal 8vo.	12¼	196	Pica, long prim., minion, & music.	.	.	Ditto	5 0	3 0

Roman Catholic schools first received parliamentary grants from December 1847 on conforming to the Management Clauses. However, as the book grant did not commence until 1847/8 the Roman Catholic and other previously excluded organizations were not at a disadvantage in this respect.

CHAPTER 3

Reading for Pleasure
1830–1860

DURING the years from 1830 to 1860 there were few outstanding children's books, but particular trends were identifiable in children's literature. There was also an awareness of the improvement in standards since 1800, although a great deal of poorly written material was available.

Boys' and girls' stories were being written in which the morals were not dominant. Examples of such work were Ann Fraser-Tytler's *Tales of the Great and Brave* (1838), Catherine Sinclair's *Holiday House* (1839) (Fig. 15), Captain Marryat's *The Children of the New Forest* (1847) and *Masterman Ready* (1848), W. H. G. Kingston's *Peter the Whaler* (1851), Charles Kingsley's *Westward Ho!* (1855), Thomas Hughes' *Tom Brown's School Days* (1856), and Charlotte M. Yonge's *The Daisy Chain* (1856).

Henry Cole (Felix Summerly), who later became Secretary of the Science and Art Department, published his *Home Treasury* (1841) in 12 booklets which contained nursery stories. Collected editions of fairy tales included Mary Howitt's translation of Hans Andersen's *Wonderful Stories for Children* (1846), Anthony Montalba's *Fairy Tales of All Nations* (1849); Annie Keary's *Tales from Asgard* (1857), J. R. Planché's *Four and Twenty French Fairy Tales* (1858), and Sir George Dasent's *Popular Tales from the North* (1859).

Original works of fantasy were represented by John Ruskin's *The King of the Golden River* (1851), W. M. Thackeray's *The Rose and The Ring* (1855), and Frances Browne's *Granny's Wonderful Chair* (1857). The period was also notable for Edward Lear's *Book*

Fig. 15. Title page from Catherine Sinclair's *Holiday House*. 1839.

of Nonsense (1846), Mrs. Gatty's *Parables from Nature* (1855), and Charles Kingsley's *The Heroes* (1856).

The tractarian movement replaced Calvinism as an influence on literature for children in these years, particularly in the work of Charlotte M. Yonge. Anglo-Catholic ideas were evident in *The Heir of Redclyffe* (1853) (Fig. 16) and in *The Daisy Chain* (1856); and were discernible in her historical novels, such as *The Little Duke* (1854). Young people were no longer regarded as sinners but as little angels, who far from requiring any conversion themselves converted their elders through their unconscious virtue. Richard, the little duke himself, typified the changed attitude.

Numerous family stories were imported from the United States which exercised a highly moral influence, such as Elizabeth Wetherell's *The Wide, Wide World* (1851), and *Queechy* (1852); Harriet Beecher Stowe's *Uncle Tom's Cabin* (1852); and Maria Cummins' *The Lamplighter* (1854). *The Wide, Wide World* was second only in popularity to *Uncle Tom's Cabin* with mid-Victorian children. Routledge alone sold approximately 80,000 copies of the former, whilst of the latter, 150,000 copies were sold within 6 months of its publication. Fantasy was represented by Nathaniel Hawthorne's *Wonder Book* (1852) and *Tanglewood Tales* (1853). Publishers attained phenomenal successes in their sales of pirated editions. Working people were able to purchase them by virtue of their low cost, whereas the originals would have been too expensive. In a period of 30 years over 7 million copies were sold by Thomas Tegg of work by Samuel Goodrich. It should not be assumed that all popular American works were pirated, as British publishers paid Harriet Beecher Stowe a proportion of their profits. Throughout the 19th century, however, the piracy was reciprocated, and in the United States the most popular books were nearly all by British authors.

Non-fiction works for children were available in only small quantities. The most popular author in this category was Rev. J. G. Wood, who wrote books on natural history. His understanding of his subject was displayed in his *Common Objects of the Sea-shore* (1857), *Common Objects of the Country* (1858), and *The*

THE

HEIR OF REDCLYFFE

BY

CHARLOTTE M. YONGE

ILLUSTRATED BY KATE GREENAWAY.

London

MACMILLAN AND CO., Limited

NEW YORK: THE MACMILLAN COMPANY

1898

Fig. 16. Title page from Charlotte M. Yonge's *The Heir of Redclyffe*. 1898 edition.

Boys' Own Book of Natural History (1860). It was only with difficulty that Routledge was able to meet the demand for *Common Objects of the Country*, which was printed in an edition of 100,000 copies, all of which were sold by the end of the first week. For many years this latter book was in continuous demand. The significance of these sales is realized when it is understood that in the field of adult publishing in the 19th century, the disposal of 50,000 copies in one year placed a book in the "best seller" class.

It is generally agreed that children are influenced favourably or otherwise by the physical appearance of the books they read. As technical improvements took place in the 18th century, it became customary for slim volumes to be produced in stiff paper covers coloured in grey or yellow. Many of the books were issued without covers of any kind, and it was for this reason that large numbers of them disintegrated and did not survive for succeeding generations. John Harris pioneered improved standards and his books appeared in attractive formats of approximately 4 inches square, and were printed in large type with numerous illustrations.

Technical progress in the 19th century was related to the growing literacy and the consequent demand for reading matter, which necessitated the production of larger editions more quickly than hitherto. Cloth-binding was invented in the late 1820's and gold was first blocked on it in 1832. These features were extended to children's books in which the most popular colours were red, blue, and green embellished with designs in gold. Type faces at that time were clear but possessed no aesthetic merit, and the formats of books continued to be square-shaped.

Steam replaced hand printing in the years between 1830 and 1860. Hand-made paper was replaced by mechanical wood (1840), by chemical wood (1854), and by esparto (1860). These innovations drastically reduced the cost of paper although in the cases of mechanical wood and esparto they did not contribute to an improved appearance in children's books.

The mid-century practice of printing novels in two or three volumes was sometimes followed in books for children. It has been suggested by Percy Muir (p. 110) that such work could not have been intended for young people. However, numerous books for this age group made their first appearance in more than one volume, including Marryat's *Masterman Ready*, Kingsley's *Westward Ho!*, Sherwood's *History of the Fairchild Family*, all in three volumes; and Marryat's *The Children of the New Forest*, and Yonge's *The Heir of Redclyffe* in two volumes.

Joseph Cundall, the publisher, issued a number of small-sized volumes in the 1840's, the covers of which were emerald, orange, cobalt, gold, and crimson. His *History of Tom Hickathrift the Conqueror* was bound in blue and gold. Other stories published by Cundall, which were also derived from the chapbook repertoire, included *Bevis of Southampton* and *Guy of Warwick*. There can be no doubt that, physically, these books were more suitable for handling by children than the two and three deckers.

A further physical feature which could enhance the appearance of a book was the use of illustrations. During the 18th and early 19th centuries, children's books contained crude woodcuts which were used continuously and in differing contexts until they were worn out. There were some painted pictures but very few reached a high artistic standard. Rowlandson, a master of the grotesque, was a representative artist of the period.

Hand-tinted engravings became very popular and lithography (1798) was often used in children's books. Harris' publications, however, contained engravings made from copper plates. In the early 1830's George Baxter began to produce prints in colour, but his work was considered to be too expensive for children's books. Darton of Holborn Hill was the first to use the process in juvenile literature, the earliest known example being the frontispiece to Mrs. Sherwood's *Caroline Mordaunt* (1835). The Baxter process was also used in *The Peter Parley Annual* for 1835.

The first outstanding illustrator of children's books was George Cruikshank who was responsible for the lively black and white drawings in the first English edition of Grimm's *Fairy Tales* (1823/6). Other prominent illustrators were Richard Doyle and John Leech, whilst in the 1840's work was undertaken by C. A. Cope, J. C. Horsley, Frederick Tayler, T. Webster, and others, many of whom contributed to Cole's *Home Treasury*. The vast majority of illustrations in children's books, however, between 1830 and 1860 were "stodgy and sham theatrical" (Darton).

Between 1828 and 1853 the average price of complete adult books declined from 16*s.* to 8*s.* 4½*d.*, or in terms of single volumes from 12*s.* 1*d.* to 7*s.* 2½*d.* Captain Marryat complained in 1838 that the price of books was too high, a situation which discouraged their purchase by individuals, and contributed to the use made of circulating libraries, such as Cawthorn and Hutt, Miles of Islington, and Mudie. Booksellers confessed their inability to derive a livelihood from bookselling alone, and it was generally agreed that working people obtained their reading matter from itinerant hawkers. Darton issued reward books by Mrs. Sherwood at 1*d.*, which were quite attractive, but "penny dreadfuls" were even more popular. At mid-century the poor were more prosperous than in 1830, but their purchasing power was in pennies rather than in shillings.

In 1845 the R.T.S. commenced a series of monthly volumes which within a decade had become a library of 100 titles. This project was undertaken in recognition of the "growing intelligence of the times" (Hewitt), and each volume cost 6*d.* or 10*d.* However, the prices of new books for children in the 1840's were beyond the reach of the working classes. Mrs. Sherwood's complete edition of *The Fairchild Family* sold at 5*s.* per volume (1845/7), Marryat's *The Children of the New Forest*, in two volumes cost 12*s.* (1847), and Montalba's *Fairy Tales of All Nations* was 9*s.* (1849), but was later reduced to 5*s.*

Older books were cheaper. Editions of *The Pilgrim's Progress* and *Robinson Crusoe* were available at 1*s.* and 1*s.* 8*d.*, whilst Lamb's *Tales from Shakespeare* was 2*s.* 6*d.* in 1844. Pirated editions from the United States were also less expensive. In the 1830's Tegg's *Peter Parley* was 3*s.* 6*d.*, whilst in the 1840's an edition by Darton cost only 2*s.* Fenimore Cooper's *The Last of the Mohicans* cost 2*s.* 6*d.* and Washington Irving's *Sketch Book* 1*s.*

Books were less expensive in 1850 than in the "cheap book" years of 1825 to 1830, and this encouraged an interest in reading.

The average price of adult books declined by 40% between 1828 and 1853. Six-shilling reprints sold for 4s. 6d. and 6d. paperbacks for 4½d. John Murray III began his *Library of Railway Readings* in 1852, in which year Cassell's *Popular Educator* was inaugurated, and John Chapman campaigned for free trade in books. Chapman was opposed in his endeavours by Longmans and Murray, but in spite of this it was possible for discounts to be obtained of 2d. and 3d. in 1s., a facility which very few booksellers declined to offer. However, free trade caused bookselling to become unprofitable and the disappearance of shops devoted exclusively to this purpose became widespread.

New children's books after 1850 were obtainable at prices similar to those of the previous two decades. Ruskin's *The King of the Golden River* was 6s. in 1851, but was later reduced to 2s. 6d.; and Ballantyne's *The Coral Island* was 6s. (1858). Copies of older works were available at prices ranging from 1s. for *Gulliver's Travels*, Lamb's *Tales from Shakespeare*, and Mrs. Trimmer's *The History of the Robins*, to 3s. 6d. for the Simpkin edition of *Sandford and Merton* (1853) and 2s. for the Bohn edition (1860). Gordon's *School and Home Series* included *Gulliver's Travels* (8d.), *The History of the Robins* (6d.), and *Robinson Crusoe* (8d.). Simms and McIntyre's *Parlour Library* included a wide range of books at 1s. 6d. each.

Throughout this period the section of the population which became increasingly literate after 1833 was only able to purchase new books at a considerable self-sacrifice, but the cheap reprints published after 1850 were available in small quantities, at least in times of low unemployment. The country, it will be remembered, was in the throes of a long-term depression from 1814 to 1850 from which it recovered with certain exceptions during the following two decades.

Reward books became common in the 1830's, by which time the number of Sunday schools had increased. The principal publishers of this literature were the S.P.C.K. and the R.T.S. In 1856 the former organization published a book entitled *The Little Dog that Lost his Master*, in which was included a select list of

"Books Adapted for Rewards in Sunday and Other Schools". They were issued in paper covers and printed on inferior paper with poor type. Many of the books were extremely pious, frequently treatises on religious subjects, and of no literary value. It was possible to receive prizes for regular attendance, punctuality, good conduct, and success in examinations.

Where it was impossible to purchase books, the principal sources from which they could be obtained were from libraries in day and Sunday schools. Books acquired in this way were of course retained by their users only for a limited period, and will be considered in the next chapter.

CHAPTER 4

School Libraries
1830–1850

IN SPITE of financial difficulties there were numerous instances of libraries being provided in schools in and after the 1830's, both by enthusiastic managers and teachers, sometimes with the assistance of outside organizations, and sometimes from their own resources.

The idea of school libraries was by no means new and had been associated with education from the earliest times. There were libraries at Alfred's Grammar School, Winchester; and at the Minster School, York; at Jarrow and at Canterbury, in and before the Middle Ages. Ashton's *Ordinances* at Shrewsbury in 1578 include references to buildings including libraries comprising "all manner of books . . . which may be either given to the school or procured with the school money". At Cheltenham in 1586 the town purchased two dictionaries for the use of pupils which were "tied fast with little chains of iron to some convenient place in the school". In 1660 Charles Hoole in his *New Discovery of the Old Art of Teaching Schoole* provided a list of more than 250 books for the school library, and in 1678 Christopher Wase of Tonbridge School included advice to librarians in his *Considerations Concerning Free-Schools*. Wase recommended that school libraries should not be confined to dictionaries and concordances but extended to a wide range of books.

Birmingham Grammar School had a library in the 17th century, and in 1691 24*s*. was paid to the master for the purchase of books to be placed therein. There is very little known of educational practice during the 17th century, but it would appear that many schools possessed very few books at all. As it was

38

frequently impossible for grammar schools to amend their classics-dominated curricula in keeping with the demands of a mercantile nation, the decline of these schools was inevitable. During the 18th century, secondary education reached its lowest ebb and there developed a preference for private tutors for middle-class children.

The S.P.C.K. introduced lending libraries into national and parochial schools from 1831. It levied an annual *per capita* subscription of 6*d*., and encouraged the formation of libraries by grants of books to the value of £5, on condition that an equal sum was raised by each school. By 1835 the S.P.C.K. had established 2438 such libraries in England, and 33 in Wales. The R.T.S. issued an address to the public "on the subject of the formation of libraries in schools" in 1832, and in that year began a scheme of library grants to *all* "well recommended cases", so that by 1849 grants had been received by 3108 libraries in Great Britain and Ireland.

On a local level libraries were usually controlled by school managers or teachers. At King's Somborne in 1844, Rev. Richard Dawes "gave in charge to the master" of the local school "a few books" which were to be lent to the scholars, but some months later he removed them to his own home in order to ascertain their value to the children at first hand. In a letter to the Inspector of Schools in 1845, Mr. Dawes stated that his lending library was a success and consisted of 540 volumes. In contrast to this, Mr. Imray, the Superintendent of a ragged school in the Marylebone district of London, reported in 1849 the establishment of "a small library and reading-room" in which the schoolmaster acted as librarian.

The subject content of the libraries varied greatly. Those supported by the S.P.C.K. included all kinds of useful and interesting works which were sponsored by its Committee of General Literature, established in 1831. Adequate distribution of the books was ensured by the opening of a Depository at Great Queen Street, London, in 1836, from where the Society sold its publications. On the other hand, the R.T.S. restricted its books to those of a religious content, though not objecting if other material of a moral, religious or scientific character was introduced. At the industrial school in Ealing Grove, Middlesex, the library consisted of books on both religious and secular subjects. The library at King's Somborne included scripture, history, natural history, voyages and travels, and story books; and libraries in British schools consisted of books issued by the Irish Commissioners of Education, the R.T.S., and "a few miscellaneous volumes".

School libraries did not serve a common purpose. Many of them were used in curricular activity, whilst most were provided for leisure reading. In the former category, the books at the Abbey Street school in Bethnal Green, London, were used as works of reference in the general activity of the school. In 1844 it was reported that there were libraries in 29 out of approximately 120 schools in the Midlands, and it was suggested that teachers could make frequent reference in oral instruction to information contained in them, and so integrate them into the system of teaching. Almost 50% of the schools of the British Society possessed small libraries but the books were mainly for home reading; and in the ragged school at Marylebone the practice was to encourage reading on the premises "every evening but one in the week". It follows that both the British schools' libraries and the library in the ragged school were not directly connected with the work of the schools, and were functioning in a manner which would later be considered within the scope of public libraries.

It should not be inferred that the school libraries were solely for the use of children. The readers who gathered at Marylebone ranged in age from 16 to 30 or 35, although, in the main, those who attended the library were also the pupils at the school. Many of the readers were street sellers of the class described by Henry Mayhew in his survey of the London poor. In addition, the term "school library" was often used for collections of books which were not intended for children, but for the instruction of the school master. The library in the British school at Harp Alley, Farringdon Street, London, was an example of this practice.

The assessable value of the libraries varied enormously from one school to another although intangible influences of particular books on individuals could be as potent in a poorly stocked library as in a well considered, numerically adequate selection. It was desirable of course that the size and relevance of collections should be related to the numbers and needs of children.

R.T.S. libraries ranged in size from 100 to 200 or more volumes, mainly of a religious nature. Seymour Tremenheere, one of the first two Inspectors of Schools, referred to a British school in London in 1842 which contained 195 pupils who had access to a library of only 70 volumes. Whilst such a collection was worthwhile, its size was hardly adequate for the number of children who were expected to use it. School libraries in the Midlands averaged collections of 214 volumes, and in 16 schools of 2204 pupils, during a period of 6 months, each child was estimated to have borrowed two books.

An inspector in 1844 queried the value of the libraries in schools which he visited, because he did not believe that the children always read the books which they borrowed, and still less did he believe that the books were read to any useful purpose. He criticized the fact that no link had been established between the techniques of reading and any pleasure which could be derived therefrom. Another inspector complained of the unsatisfactory content of school libraries in the West country, where the books consisted of uninteresting matter "far above the comprehension of children".

In contrast, Rev. Richard Dawes noted with pleasure the extent to which some of the children at King's Somborne had profited from the books which he had provided, and attempted to cater for the reading interests of each individual. This meaningful selection of material resulted in the books being discussed among the children and frequent requests were made for particular books on their return to the library. Books which were popular included *Evenings at Home* in which "the best stories are still well worth reading" (Darton), *The Pilgrim's Progress*, and Sir James Barrow's account of the seizure of the Bounty, neither of the latter two volumes being written specifically for children.

The demand for, and the provision of, school libraries usually sprang from religious bodies with an interest in education, and from individuals who believed in the importance of reading. In addition, the provision of libraries in schools was sometimes encouraged by inspectors appointed by the Committee of Council on Education. There is very little evidence of interest being taken by individuals not directly concerned with formal education, although a plea was made for school libraries by Edward Edwards of the British Museum in his evidence to the *Select Committee on Public Libraries* in 1849. He recommended that "lending libraries of a good kind should be connected with schools" (p. 25). It is not clear from the context whether he envisaged them as lending libraries for their districts or for the sole use of pupils and staff in the schools. It is perhaps at this point, however, that one can discern the beginnings of a connection between school libraries and the public library movement.

Even where school libraries were adequate to the needs of their users, very few children benefited from their existence. As late as 1852, 60% of the children in England and Wales between the ages of 3 and 15 were not at school, and of the 2 million who received a formal education, 42% were in attendance for less than one year. Therefore, whilst the importance of libraries varied in different schools as regards size and content in their ability to assist the growth of literacy in children, their influence was only extended to a minority.

It is reasonable to suggest that the growth of libraries in schools from 1831 was related to the more general spirit of educational and social reform which prevailed in this country during the years immediately following the Parliamentary Reform Act of 1832.

Day schools were not the only places which possessed libraries for the use of children. Many Sunday schools contained collections. The R.T.S. address to the public on the establishment of libraries in 1832 referred as much to their formation in Sunday schools as in day schools, and it was regarded as quite as important to promote the cause of education in the former as in the latter.

The only education which thousands of children received was in the Sunday schools, and in the period under discussion numerous small collections of books had been acquired by these bodies both in towns and villages, and the books were made available for home reading. As with day school libraries, those in Sunday schools varied greatly from one to another. In South Wales in 1839 the instruction conveyed was restricted "by the want of books", whilst in Derbyshire in 1842 the Inspector of Schools expressed satisfaction with those libraries he saw. In London nearly every church and chapel had a Sunday school library for the children, most of them containing material of a religious character, although some included secular books of voyages and travels. A reading room attached to the Liverpool Domestic Mission's Tuckerman Institute in 1850 was open every evening to about 100 young people, and on Mondays it was usual for approximately 70 volumes to be borrowed for home reading.

Where Sunday school libraries existed their influence was potentially great, in furthering the education of the 3 million children in England and Wales who did not attend day school. There was a point of view, however, which advocated small collections for the use of teachers, many of whom were enthusiastic but deficient in biblical knowledge and not sufficiently literate to teach children. A good teachers' collection would include books on the particular subjects taught at the school, and a selection of reference books. This would be made possible by weekly or monthly subscriptions from the teachers, an allocation of money from the school fund, and contributions from well-wishers. A library of this kind, consisting of 360 volumes, was formed in 1850 at the Hanover Square Sunday schools in Newcastle upon Tyne.

It would be impossible to determine to what extent Sunday school libraries were provided for the use of children, and the presence of such libraries did not necessarily contribute directly to the growth of literacy among young people.

CHAPTER 5

The Stagnant Years in Education
1850–1870

THE decade 1842–52 saw the parliamentary grant for educational purposes raised from £40,000 to £160,000 per year, and in 1856 an Education Department was established. The long-term depression, however, was followed by a boom during the two succeeding decades, in which there was a diminution of the social tension and also of educational reform. It has been said that although the Great Exhibition of 1851 served to crystallize the immense possibilities of the future, it "was in some respects the pageant of an epoch already passing away" (Woodward). As late as 1864, Lord Palmerston considered that in domestic affairs "there is really nothing to be done. We cannot", he said, "go on adding to the Statute Book . . . ", and in this he enjoyed the general support of his party.

In 1858 the Minutes of the Committee of Council were consolidated and reduced to form a code. It was specified in Article 4 of the Code of 1860 that "the object of the grant is to promote the education of children belonging to the class who support themselves by manual labour". Schools could only be assisted if they were associated with a recognized religious denomination or if "the Scriptures are read daily from the Authorized Version" (Article 8) in addition to secular instruction. Grants were available only to schools which were open to inspection (Article 13).

The Newcastle Commission on *The State of Popular Education in England* (1858) reported in 1861. It had considered the measures which would be required for the extension of sound and cheap elementary instruction, and decided that it was necessary to institute an examination in schools, on the results of which the position of teachers would depend. These proposals were made effective in the Revised Code of 1862. In a parliamentary speech, Robert Lowe, the Vice-President of the Committee of Council, promised "that this system shall be either the one thing or the other; if it is not cheap it shall be efficient, if it is not efficient it shall be cheap". Subject to annual modifications the Revised Code remained in force for elementary schools until 1871.

In 1868 the Taunton Commission reported its findings. It was concerned with schools not investigated by the Newcastle Commission, or by the Clarendon Commission (1864) which had investigated the nine schools of Charterhouse, Eton, Harrow, Merchant Tailors, Rugby, St. Paul's, Shrewsbury, Westminster, and Winchester. The Taunton Commissioners discovered that the only grammar schools providing a high standard of free education to a large number of scholars were at Bedford, Birmingham, and Manchester, whilst other schools in this category offered "a similar education to that which may be obtained in our National and British schools". There was an urgent need for good schools which would cater for children aged 14 or 15, and it was suggested that such schools should either be attached to elementary schools which were subject to inspection, or that they should be brought into some relationship one with another. It should be possible for promising boys in elementary schools to be promoted without an increased payment being required from parents. As a result of the Taunton Commission Report, the Endowed Schools Act was passed in 1869 which revitalized the endowed grammar schools.

Educational development in the elementary sector between 1833 and 1870 was implemented virtually without legislation, but through the agency of departmental Minutes. Numerous attempts were made in 1843, 1853, 1855, 1867, and 1868, to improve the facilities which were available, but in each case they proved abortive in the face of opposition from religious organizations. It may be inferred from the regularity with which the topic was raised, that there was a growing movement favourable to popular education.

In many of the manufacturing towns, only a minority of children obtained education of any kind, and in 1852 extremely few aged 12 or more would be found at school. There were in 1851, 13,879 "dames' schools" in England and Wales, the majority of which functioned for the supervision of children whilst their parents were at work, but could not be regarded as places of instruction. In the Census of 1851, more than 700 heads of such schools certified their returns with a mark.

Approximately $1\frac{1}{2}$ million children in 1870 were on the registers of inspected schools, but at a conservative estimate an equal number attended either establishments which were completely unsuitable for educational purposes, or no schools of any kind. An inquiry into Liverpool schools for poorer children in 1869 revealed that 25% were in the former category and another 25% in the latter. The Education Act of 1870 was intended to remedy this situation.

In addition to the day schools sponsored by the societies there were developments in factory and evening schools. Factory schools were not provided in all industrial areas, and there were no such establishments in 1858 in the mining districts of Durham and Cumberland. Where these schools existed it was frequently discovered that the children were not occupied educationally, but their presence was certified as school attendance, and in statistical returns they were regarded as being under instruction. Miners demanded schools for their children similar to those which they believed to be available in factories, but where experiments were made, the children were often too exhausted to profit from the facilities.

In 1864 a Factories Regulation Act standardized educational provision, which was in 1867 extended to almost all forms of manual labour with the exception of agriculture. The hours to be worked by children were limited to a half-day with an obligation of daily attendance at school. Every child between the ages of 8 and 13 who worked in a factory was to spend half the day (6 a.m.

to 12 noon, or 1 p.m. to 6 p.m.) in the mill, and the other half (1.30 p.m. to 4.30 p.m. or 9 a.m. to 12 noon) at school. The half-time system appeared to be successful and was widely adopted in the large factory towns of Lancashire.

Evening schools continued to exert a positive influence, and were to be encountered in industrial areas such as Liverpool and the Potteries. They were not popular in agricultural and mining districts as the distances to be travelled were too great in the case of the former, and they were not convenient to the working schedules of colliery labour. In Wales the evening schools were uncommon. During the 1860's, however, there was evidence that their numbers were increasing in various places such as Gloucester-shire and Herefordshire where they continued the instruction which had been commenced in day schools, but which had been terminated as the children reached the age of 10 years.

The influence of Sunday schools in secular education declined substantially between 1850 and 1870. In the Census of 1851 returns were received from 23,137 Sunday schools as opposed to 44,836 day schools. Their religious objectives were discussed in the Newcastle Report, and they were regarded as the means by which the various denominations extended their numbers.

Between 1851 and 1861 the illiteracy rate for men fell from 30·7% to 24·6%, and for women from 45·2% to 34·7% (Cole). It is sometimes extremely difficult, however, to show the full measure of improvement. The percentage of children in Middlesex who could read letters and monosyllables but were unable to read simple narratives fell from 39·72% in 1850 to 27·93% in 1853, but there was in fact real progress. The apparent deterioration was due to the inclusion from 1851 of statistics relating to infants. The reading of younger scholars was in need of special attention which it did not receive.

An ability to recognize letters and words of one syllable could hardly render a child literate, and it was therefore necessary for the teaching of reading to become a matter of fundamental importance. In the later 1850's it was not uncommon in British and Wesleyan schools in the north for at least 75% of the children to read books of general interest with fluency, but even in the highest standards there was an almost complete absence of expression. Standards of reading improved rapidly in the Church schools of Chester, Shropshire, and Stafford. Whilst in 1859 the inspector estimated that 25% of the children could read passably a book such as the 3rd Irish Reader, in 1861 he found that 33% of them could read fairly well from their accustomed book, and 8% could read whatever suitable book was placed before them.

The principal reasons for poor reading ability were considered to be irregularity of attendance; the advanced age at which children first attended school, particulary in factory districts where many parents only sent their children when they were coerced by the Factory Act; and uncultured homes where the vernacular varied so much from standard English that a reading lesson presented the difficulties normally encountered in the learning of a foreign language.

James Currie, the Principal of the Church of Scotland Training College at Edinburgh, suggested standards of attainment which should be reached by children at elementary school. On leaving a good infants' school at the age of 7 years, a child should be able to read with fluency easy narratives and the simpler parts of the Bible, and having progressed further should be capable of reading accounts in newspapers, either silently or orally. The qualities of good reading were defined by Currie as purity of diction, correct accent, emphasis, deliberation, correct pitch, modulation, and fluency. He was of his period in considering it essential for children to be sufficiently acquainted with the Bible to understand the allusions and arguments used by a clergyman in a sermon, and to remember from their study of the Catechism the duties of man to both God and his neighbour. If children attended school until they were 11 years of age, they should "learn thoroughly well all the absolute essentials of education" so that in later years they might continue to instruct themselves. '

Unfortunately most children did not have the opportunity to attend school for 6 years. In a report of a *Conference on School*

Attendance in 1857, it was estimated that of 2 million children at school:

42% attended less than 1 year
22% attended 1 or less than 2 years
15% attended 2 or less than 3 years
9% attended 3 or less than 4 years
5% attended 4 or less than 5 years
4% attended 5 or less than 6 years

The Census returns of 1851 showed that the majority of children in elementary schools were taught only the three R's. After 1852, however, a movement grew to include subjects in addition to reading, writing and arithmetic in the school curriculum, and it became increasingly customary for drawing, English history, etymology, geography, and other subjects to be taught. These innovations were not distributed evenly throughout schools, and whilst the upper standards received a surfeit of geography and history, the lower sections of schools were restricted to reading and spelling. This progress was, however, undermined following the introduction of the Revised Code.

CHAPTER 6

Books in Schools
1850–1870

THE numbers of textbooks continued to increase and were issued by almost every educational society. Grammar books were available in large quantities and were modelled on a variety of systems. Matthew Arnold advocated the adoption of chosen texts and looked to the Committee of Council to select suitable books. It is curious that he was not so much concerned with the relative merits of books as with the need to standardize their use in schools.

An inspector of Roman Catholic schools in 1858 concurred with Arnold in his view that no books had been published which were so superior that they were widely adopted by school managers. Another inspector, however, complained that there was an insufficient variety of books, but it is possible that he was referring to their suitability for elementary schools.

The five Reading Books compiled and published under the authority of the Irish Commissioners were extensively used in both the National and the British schools of England and Wales. These books propounded in simple language the qualities of good workmen, and the advantages of industry and thrift as envisaged by the upper class. The series was unfavourably criticized by an Assistant Commissioner in the report of the Newcastle Commission. He considered that the lowest classes in Ireland were more advanced educationally than their counterparts in England, a fact which rendered unsuitable the use of the Readers in English schools. The style was beyond the comprehension of children in the northern counties, and the sentences were too long and complicated for pupils unaccustomed to sustained thought.

The standards and speed of printing had improved greatly in

the 1840's so that in the following decade, publishers were becoming involved in the mass production of books. William Collins II issued his first school atlas in 1856 and was later appointed publisher to the Scottish School Book Association and the Irish National Schools. In a period of 10 years he provided the latter body with 2,320,500 copies of 31 books. Other publishers who were successful in the educational field in these years were Cassell (*Primary Series*), Chambers (*Educational Course*), Constable (*Educational Series*), Darton (*School Library*), Gleig (*School Series*), and Simpkin Marshall (*School and Home Series*). Among the productions of the latter were Dr. Clyde's *Elementary Geography* (1*s.* 6*d.*), Dr. Clyde's *School Geography* (4*s.*), William Lawson's *Geography of the British Empire* (3*s.*) and J. D. Morell's *Poetical Reading Book*.

A recurring disadvantage of school books was their unsuitability for the children before whom they were placed. Some were far too difficult, whilst others were arid and failed to arouse interest in their readers. Geography books consisted of lists of names and measurements rather than contents which would both interest and inform children. With the possible exception of the Bible, the school reading book of many children formed the only literature to which they had access, and if this was solely factual, then they were deprived of imaginative reading of any kind. Unfortunately many reading books contained the work of incompetent authors and were feeble, inaccurate, and colourless. Such writers actually stultified children's taste, when they were the only possible agency for its development. It was to be deplored that in spite of the vast resources of English literature, Victorian children in elementary schools were provided with inferior poetical extracts. Matthew Arnold in his report for 1867 quoted a piece of doggerel which he had found in a book for pupils in Standard V which included:

> She is a rich and rare land.
>   Oh! she is a fresh and fair land.
> She is a dear and rare land.
>   This native land of mine.

No men than hers are braver,
    The women's hearts ne'er waver;
I'd freely die to save her
    And think my lot divine.

She's not a dull or cold land.
    No, she's a warm and bold land;
Oh! she's a true and old land.
    This native land of mine.

The ability to read with intelligence, accuracy, and taste was no easy task, and it was impossible for a child to attain success unless the book he used was suited to his understanding and calculated to awaken his interest.

Dr. Currie considered that it was necessary for the contents of the books to be graduated in order to afford the children sufficient practice in each stage of their progress. Other features which he advocated were clarity of thought and expression, a balance of statement and example, and the inclusion of a wide variety of topics presented in an interesting manner.

It was quite common for children to be taught to read by the alphabetic method, but that was not the only scheme which was recognized. Kay-Shuttleworth's volume which made use of phonics has been described. Dr. Currie drew attention to a method which

> employs for a time a different alphabet, in which the characters are sufficiently numerous to denote all the sounds of the language, and have uniform power . . . The reading lessons are written in these characters, until the child acquired the habit of regularly associating the sound of each letter with the sign of it. The transition is made to the common alphabetic characters by giving him the same primers to read in them as he has already been reading in the phonetic characters.

He advocated the use of "Look and Say" which he thought was free from the objections raised against phonics. Mrs. E. M. Field criticized a volume published in 1869 in which letters were crossed through and marked diacritically so that polysyllables could be read without difficulty (Field, p. 338).

A number of inspectors were highly critical of the content of the traditional reading books regardless of the method by which they facilitated reading. In some schools reading lessons were rendered interesting by the introduction of *The Pilgrim's Progress*, *Robinson Crusoe*, and *The Swiss Family Robinson*. It was believed that this practice would be widely imitated if such books were made available at the prices of normal school books. The introduction of books of this kind in cheap editions would bring about an improvement in the reading of younger children. One inspector considered that "half an hour of *Sir Roger de Coverley* or *Robinson Crusoe* or Cowper's *The Task*, would be worth hours of lessons on natural history or descriptive geography". Simpkin Marshall's illustrated *School and Home Series* was a bid to satisfy this new demand, and was designed "to place interesting and attractive books within the reach of schools and school libraries". *The Child's Story Book* sold in four parts, each at 2*d.*, and included well known tales from Aesop, *The Arabian Nights*, Andersen, Grimm, and Perrault. In the same series could be obtained Defoe's *Robinson Crusoe* at 8*d.*, Maria Edgeworth's *Lame Jervas* and *Tomorrow* at 4*d.*, Lamb's *Tales from Shakespeare* in four parts at 3*d.*, and Mrs. Trimmer's *The History of the Robins* at 8*d.*

During the 1850's insufficient money was spent on books, and in 1852 only 8 ·3 % of the income of schools was allocated to their purchase. In a school of 200 children it was calculated that rather more than £40 should be spent on books and apparatus. It was not uncommon for two children simultaneously to learn their reading from one book, and in a Herefordshire school of 76 children in 1861 the stock of religious reading books consisted of three torn Bibles, whilst books of a secular character were not available. In many of the humblest schools in the remote districts of North Wales, however, there appeared to be reasonable quantities of books published by the British Society, the Irish Commissioners, and the National Society. Schools in South Wales were also well provided, but in both areas there appeared to be no policy in the selection and acquisition of books. An inspector of British schools contrasted the situation at mid-century, when in most schools the Bible was the only reading book, with 1860, when books written in a readable style, upon the subjects of every-day life, were easily accessible.

Where books were not provided by the schools it was fairly common for children to purchase their own copies. School children at Bosbury, Redditch, Nuneaton, and Worcester, obtained their own books in the early 1850's. At Nuneaton it was reported that no difficulty had been encountered in children providing secular books whilst the school was responsible for religious literature. An outstanding example was cited at the Sunningdale National school. Between January and June 1852, 46 children from 37 families purchased 95 lesson books and works of reference to the amount of £1 19s. 4d. The average outlay for each family was 1s. 0¾d., and in almost every instance considerable effort was necessary on the part of parents so that their children could obtain the necessary books. The following table is a record of the transaction which also indicates the titles in use at that time.

January to June, 1852

	Each	Total
33 *Etymology*, Ross	3d.	8s. 3d.
18 *Sacred Geography*	1¼d.	1s. 10½d.
10 *Spelling Books*	6¾d.	5s. 7½d.
12 Crossley's *Arithmetic*	10d.	10s.
7 Allen & Cornwell's *English Grammar*	10d.	5s. 10d.
3 Reid's *Dictionary*	2s. 2d.	6s. 6d.
12 *Easy Lessons in Arithmetic*	1¼d.	1s. 3d.
		£1 19s. 4d.

Matthew Arnold reported that in many British and Wesleyan schools where books were not provided, several children had none, and it would cause intolerable hardship if their purchase were made obligatory. An Inspector of national schools in the eastern counties referred to boys who were detained in lower standards than was warranted by their intelligence because they were unable to procure the required books. In contrast he referred to a boy who regardless of his abilities was placed in the top class because his parents insisted on providing books which were beyond the intelligence of the child. Arnold considered that all schools should possess a public stock of books from which children would be supplied if they could not acquire them for themselves.

The List of Books issued by the Committee of Council and the capitation grants for books were found to be of valuable assistance, but it was regretted that the addition of new books to the former was not undertaken more frequently. It seemed reasonable to many that managers should be enabled to select any books published by educational societies recognized by the Committee. The total expenditure from educational grants in Great Britain from 1839 to 1870 was £12,546,559, of which £52,521 was allocated to books, maps, diagrams, and scientific apparatus. Expenditure on books alone from the first grant in 1848 to 1862 was as follows:

	£		£
1848	617	1856	3957
1849	2937	1857	7808
1850	1878	1858	5718
1851	1715	1859	6145
1852	2646	1860	4833
1853	2895	1861	5992
1854	1866	1862	630
1855	2884		

It is almost impossible to calculate the book grants for England and Wales as during the period 1850–70, the Committee of Council and the Education Department administered grants for the whole of Britain.

The Code of 1860 continued to permit grants for individual items, although they were considerably reduced. The grants for books, maps and diagrams was not to exceed 10*d*. per head of the number of children in average attendance at a school, and the total cost of books ordered was not to be less than £3. In order to meet the requirements of the grant, 1*s*. 8*d*. per head was to be voluntarily subscribed by schools and it was made clear that books must be selected from the list compiled by the Committee of Council. Grants could not be raised more frequently than triennially unless the attendance increased by 25%.

A small section of the Newcastle Report dealt with the Book Department of the Committee of Council. It was argued that the Committee could be accused of censorship no matter to what extent it protested to the contrary. Many books were in circulation which contained errors and were thus unfit for use in schools, but were not condemned by the Committee of Council, whilst others did not appear in the list for the sole reason that it must be confined within reasonable limits.

Criticism was made of the administrative costs of the Book Department, which had in 1860 been in receipt of a grant of £5683. The administration of this sum required a separate office in Great George Street, Westminster, with a staff of clerks; and Messrs. Longman received a sum of £1000 for the collection, package, and transmission of the books.

The Newcastle Commission recommended that a general annual grant should supersede the various special grants, including that for books; and that the list should be withdrawn. It was hoped that booksellers would continue to allow to managers of schools the same discount which they allowed to the Government!

In accordance with the recommendations of the Newcastle Commission, grants were paid to schools on the basis of attendances and results. As has been pointed out, the purpose of the changes was partly intended to economize in government expenditure, a feature which was effective immediately. The aid from the Government towards the support of elementary schools was reduced at the rate of 3*s*. 9*d*. per scholar between 1861 and 1866; but the income of the schools from local and voluntary sources had, in the same period, increased only at the rate of 1*s*. 1*d*. per scholar.

In 1867 it was resolved to make an additional grant of 1s. 4d. per pass in reading, writing, and arithmetic, but the total must not exceed £8 for any one school, subject to conditions which included the standard of passes in schools and the adoption of a fourth subject in which at least 20% of the scholars over 6 years of age were successful. These clauses were incorporated into the Code of 1868.

The intention was to raise the standard of literacy, but after 5 years only an insignificant improvement was discernible in reading and writing, whilst in arithmetic there was a slight retrogression. The following table lists the percentages of failures in the three obligatory subjects during the period:

	1864	1865	1867
Reading	11·87	11·23	9·29
Writing	13·98	13·39	12·41
Arithmetic	23·69	23·58	23·72

It was generally agreed that the Revised Code improved the standards in the lower classes in schools, but the higher classes were allowed to stagnate. Reading was passable but not good and many children read with fluency but not intelligence. A single book was read continuously until the examination when a child could repeat the text from memory. In practice, therefore, teachers who drilled their pupils without developing their intelligence earned high capitation grants. The Revised Code discouraged all instruction except that which was compulsory in all but the most progressive schools, and scholars were neglected who were irregular in their attendance or dull. Thus the poorest, most ignorant, and migratory children did not benefit at all.

The required standards in reading were not high under the Revised Code and were as follows:

Standard I   Narrative in monosyllables
Standard II   One of the narratives next in order after monosyllables in any elementary reading book used in the school

Standard III	Short paragraph from an elementary reading book used in the school
Standard IV	Short paragraph from a more advanced reading book used in the school
Standard V	Few lines of poetry from a reading book used in the first standard in the school
Standard VI	Short ordinary paragraph in a newspaper or other modern narrative

The large-scale reductions in expenditure adversely influenced the supply of books in schools. *A Report on the Schools for the Poorer Classes of Children in Birmingham, Leeds, Liverpool and Manchester* in 1869 revealed a depressing situation. At Birmingham the teachers had no means of determining what books should be used and no supply of their own. There was scarcely one good school at Leeds where the children came "in time to read and write after a fashion". Attendance at many Manchester schools was "scarcely, if at all, to be preferred to vagrancy". The quality of education in Liverpool was even worse and in one school of 17 children there were only 10 books, 6 of which differed from one another.

It is true, however, that between 1860 and 1870 the school textbook developed significantly, but writers and publishers required evidence of increased demand to induce them to devote their attention to the production of relevant primers. The Newcastle Commission had envisaged such a prospect, and whilst Matthew Arnold condemned the results of the Revised Code, he believed that the new system had stimulated the production of a better and more meaningful type of reading book.

In 1863 Arnold drew attention to some of the more unfortunate features in school books which he thought were in process of being superseded. He quoted such sentences as:

> The crocodile is viviparous . . .
> Quicksilver, antimony, calamine, zinc, etc. are metals . . .
> The slope of a desk is oblique, the corners of the door are angles . . .
> Some time after one meal is digested we feel again the sensation of hunger, which is gratified by again taking food . . .

Arnold considered that some of the newer books even went to extremes in an endeavour to avoid aridity and pedantry; and contained "rather too many abbreviations, too many words meant to imitate the noises of animals, and too much of that part of human utterance which may be called the interjectional".

There were many excellent series of books but they tended to be inappropriate to the abilities of English children. On the other hand, several series were poorly presented and contained large numbers of errors. An inspector in 1869 remarked that he found it impossible to describe the contempt he felt for "the twaddle, false moral, and degraded sentimentality, which some people consider fit to form the education of the working classes". Another expressed the view that there were no thoroughly good reading books in use, and inferred that biblical extracts were still in circulation for the teaching of reading.

There was a consequent demand for government control over the choice of books to be used in grant-aided schools. It seemed reasonable to many inspectors that the Committee of Council should at least have the power to reject books which were patently unfit for educational use. Matthew Arnold pointed out that in Germany, school books were controlled by qualified educationists in particular subjects, and recommended that this example should be followed in England instead of "either exercising this control with imperfect instruments, or abandoning it altogether".

CHAPTER 7

School and Public Libraries
1850–1870

THE reading facilities in elementary day schools and Sunday schools were given some attention in the Newcastle Report. Whilst there is not a great deal of information available, it seems evident that Sunday schools often possessed superior libraries to day schools. In East Anglia "nearly every Sunday school" had a library which on the whole was "well used" by 25–50% of the scholars. Lending libraries in Bradford and Rochdale frequently contained "several hundred volumes for free circulation amongst the teachers and scholars". Most of the books were religious in content but recently opened libraries included "a considerable number of amusing works, stories, travels and the like".

In contrast there was a "great want of good school libraries" in East Anglia, and in South London where they were "so rare as almost to be unknown". Managers in some Liverpool schools had formed and maintained school libraries with the aid of the capitation grant. It is surprising that this practice was not more widespread, since the Committee of Council book grants were introduced after 1847. However, the Committee did not extend its generosity indefinitely as has been shown.

Perhaps the most encouraging library activity during the 1850's was the establishment of a collection at St. Martin's school, Worcester, which was begun with a few books provided by the teacher. He observed the interest his project aroused among the boys and suggested that they should raise funds for the purchase of more books. They subscribed 32s. to which the teacher added £10, together with a grant of £5 from the S.P.C.K. It was possible to assemble thus a well chosen collection. Apart from this the only voice to be heard was that of Rev. M. Mitchell, H.M.I. for the eastern counties, who in 1855 called for government grants for school libraries. Some school libraries were formed in Yorkshire but they were intended for community use in the districts concerned.

The Revised Code of 1862 discouraged all instruction above the three elementary subjects, a situation which militated against a wide use of books and was not conducive to the spread of libraries. During the years between 1850 and 1870 there is very little evidence of school library development in this country. The negative policies which operated in the broad field of education apparently stifled enthusiasm in every sector of academic activity.

There were very few library facilities available in these years apart from those which were provided by day and Sunday schools. It is true that some provision was made in the libraries of Mechanics' Institutes, and in Birmingham there was such a collection as early as 1797 in which was contained some material for young people.

An Anglican curate formed a library in London in 1848 for the residents of White Hart Court in Whitcomb Street. With the assistance of donations of books and small monetary subscriptions he assembled a collection of approximately 400 volumes, which included children's books. The members consisted of working people who were admitted on payment of 1d. per week. At the end of the first 3 months there were 143 subscribers, but when the curate left the parish, the library did not survive. In 1849 it was reported that there were no public libraries in London for the use of the working classes. It has been shown that individual enthusiasm was not sufficient to sustain school libraries, and the outcome at Whitcomb Street serves to emphasize the point with respect to public libraries.

In 1849 *The Report from the Select Committee on Public Libraries* was published. The recommendation was made that public libraries "should be based on a firm and durable foundation; that they should be freely accessible to all the public; that they should be open during the evenings, and that they should, as far as possible, be lending libraries".

The importance of evening opening was stressed because the working people were unable to use libraries at any other time. The British Museum in London, and the Chetham Library in Manchester both closed at 4 p.m., because they were not equipped with artificial lighting. The view prevailed that unshielded gas light was injurious to the bindings of books, although this had not been born out in libraries in the United States, where gas lighting had been installed. *The Select Committee* advocated gas lighting in public libraries after it had accumulated sufficient favourable evidence.

The first Public Libraries Act was passed in 1850. It became possible for local government areas with populations exceeding 10,000 to adopt the Act if they so wished. The rate which could be levied for the provision and maintenance of the libraries was limited to $\frac{1}{2}d.$ in the pound, and admission was to be free. No provision was made for the purchase of books as it was considered that adequate donations of material would be made. The Public Libraries Act of 1855 repealed that of 1850. Under its terms the population limit was reduced to 5000, the amount of rate was increased from $\frac{1}{2}d.$ to $1d.$, and the purchase, provision and repair of books was authorized. In view of the financial limitations it is not surprising that by 1859 only 21 local authorities had adopted the Act.

The earliest known example of a service being provided for children in a rate-supported library was at Manchester in 1862. A separate reading department for boys with its own stock of suitably selected literature was recommended by the librarian in 1858, and this proposal was approved by the local Library Committee in 1861. It was not considered necessary to cater for girls.

In 1865, Richard Hinton, the librarian of Birkenhead, made special provision of children's books. Some students of the history of children's libraries have held the mistaken opinion that the service at Birkenhead was the earliest example of its kind, but there can be no doubt that the pioneering library was at Manchester.

The initial reason for facilities being made at Manchester was due to the heavy use of the library by unemployed artisans in a time of economic depression which was eventually aggravated by the cotton famine which had been brought about by the American Civil War. It became desirable to separate the boys from the adult readers.

There is evidence that in 1869 the collections at Birmingham Public Library included "juvenile books" at the central department and at two branches. This appears to be the only public library of the period to follow the recommendations of *The Select Committee* of 1849, in making available its books for home reading.

Whilst the activity was praiseworthy at Birkenhead, Birmingham, and Manchester, the numbers of books were not always adequate to meet any appreciable demand. At Birkenhead, 743 books were issued to children in 1865, and this was increased to 2608 in 1870. The population of the town was 45,000 in 1871, and it can be estimated therefore that there were approximately 7500 children if a calculation is made on the basis of one child to every five adults. However, the whole child population, even had it been completely literate, could not have used the library at one time, and in view of this the size of the collection at Birkenhead was probably satisfactory.

There were 456 children's books at Birmingham in 1869, which were distributed between the central lending library (298) and two branches (43 and 115). The total bookstock held by the Birmingham libraries was 50,300 volumes. The number of children's books which were issued in 1868 was 8861, mainly from the central library, whilst the total issues for that year were 306,767. In 1871 the population of Birmingham was 344,000 of which approximately 69,000 would be children. The inadequacy of 456 books for a community of this size cannot be gainsaid, even when it is taken into consideration that in 1870 only 42·3% of the working-class population of this country between the ages of 3 and 12 was receiving formal instruction. Educational provision at Birmingham was not above the national average.

The views which were expressed by many librarians as to what was suitable for children showed a degree of understanding of their needs which was not usual in those days. At Manchester the books included *The Arabian Nights*, Aesop's *Fables*, *Robinson Crusoe*, and Charles Dickens' *A Child's History of England*. Books which were popular at Birmingham included Mrs. Carey-Brock's *Margaret's Secret*, Mrs. S. C. Hall's *Union Jack*, Hans Andersen's *The Silver Shilling*, Mark Lemon's *Tom Moody's Tales*, McIntosh's *Evenings at Donaldson Manor*, Routledge's *Handbook of Cricket*, and Mary Howitt's *The Two Apprentices*.

It is impossible to estimate the value of the library facilities to the young people. Many of the users were in attendance at school or had left recently. They had been taught the mechanics of reading but had not developed the ability to understand what they read. It was not uncommon for them to choose books by their titles from the catalogue, and after a brief scrutiny to return them unread. As librarians became aware of the need for guidance they frequently contacted the schools in order to obtain the co-operation of teachers.

CHAPTER 8

The Golden Years of Children's Literature Part I 1860–1890

THE publishers who dominated the scene for most of the period under discussion were Macmillan and Routledge. The former had been in financial difficulties in the 1850's but the situation changed quickly with the success of Kingsley's *Westward Ho!* and Hughes' *Tom Brown's School Days*. Writers of the calibre of Lewis Carroll, Mrs. Molesworth, Charlotte M. Yonge, and in the 1890's, Rudyard Kipling, all helped to ensure the supremacy of the house of Macmillan.

Routledge had commenced business in 1834 but did not achieve success with children's books until he became associated with Edward Lear in 1861. From the 1860's and throughout the 19th century the firm specialized in outstanding picture books by Crane, Caldecott, and Greenaway. During the middle period, however, its success was founded on the piracy of American books, an activity which will be considered later in this chapter.

Longman enjoyed an intermittent success with children's books from the publication in 1839 of Catherine Sinclair's *Holiday House*. Farrar's *Eric; or, Little By Little* was also popular, and in the 1870's the acquisition of Andrew Lang maintained the status of the firm as a major publisher of books for children.

The commercial success of Nelson was achieved through the publication of books for children, among whose authors were R. M. Ballantyne and Charlotte Tucker (A.L.O.E.). In the 1870's the house of Thomas Nelson was the largest publisher of juvenile literature. Other notable publishers in the mid-Victorian period were Bell, Bohn, Chapman & Hall, Grant & Griffith, Griffith & Farran, Seeley & Burnside, Smith & Elder, and Strahan.

In the mid-Victorian period the number of children's books increased greatly. The largest group of new books published in 1870 was in religious subjects (811), but this was followed by 695 juvenile works, many of which had a religious content. After the Education Act of 1870, numerous firms became involved in publishing for children, including Cassell and Blackie. During the last two decades of the century the number of publishers increased greatly with the growth of literacy.

An inherent conservatism existed in British publishing. This was frequently reflected in a lack of confidence on the part of publishers in the sales potential of work by new authors of children's books. There appeared to be little appreciation of the features in children's books which were likely to appeal to the reading public.

Bell refused to become involved with the first series of Mrs. Gatty's *Parables from Nature* in 1855; Routledge declined to purchase the copyright of Lear's *Book of Nonsense* in 1861, but agreed to publish it on a commission basis; and Carroll's *Alice in Wonderland* was similarly treated by Macmillan in 1864.

Stevenson accepted from Cassell an offer for *Treasure Island* of a royalty of 10% on the published price, with an advance of £50 on his signing the agreement and a further £50 on publication. Cassell did not consider this to be ungenerous for a hitherto little known writer. However, the book was an immediate success, and consequently for *Kidnapped* Stevenson received an advance payment of £250. The terms of the agreements which have been described were not a source of encouragement to writers, and the attitude of publishers in this respect was surely detrimental to the development of literature for children.

In contrast, there were numerous occasions when publishers regarded themselves as fortunate to be associated with particular writers. There had been considerable competition among publishers for the work of Mrs. Sherwood earlier in the century and the solution of Macmillan's publishing problems has been described. Although Carroll did not elicit any initial enthusiasm for *Alice* from Macmillan, approximately 180,000 copies were sold in various editions between 1865 and the author's death in

THROUGH THE LOOKING-GLASS,

AND WHAT ALICE FOUND THERE.

BY

LEWIS CARROLL,

AUTHOR OF "ALICE'S ADVENTURES IN WONDERLAND."

WITH FIFTY ILLUSTRATIONS

BY JOHN TENNIEL.

THIRTIETH THOUSAND.

London:

MACMILLAN & CO.

1872.

[*The Right of Translation and Reproduction is reserved.*]

FIG. 17. Title page from Lewis Carroll's *Through the Looking Glass*. 1872.

1898. Macmillan printed 9000 copies, and in so doing, seriously underestimated the demand for *Through The Looking Glass* (Fig. 17). It was never as popular as *Alice* but by 1893 a total of 60,000 copies had been sold.

The children's books which approached the equivalent of adult best sellers were the picture books of Walter Crane, Randolph Caldecott, and Kate Greenaway. The engraving and printing costs were high and the early picture books of Crane were not an economic proposition unless it was possible to sell at least 50,000 copies of a single work. *The Baby's Opera* was bound in card-board covers and at 5*s.* the first edition of 10,000 copies was quickly exhausted. Caldecott's *The House that Jack Built* and *John Gilpin* (1878) were very popular, and by 1885, 100,000 copies had been sold. Kate Greenaway's *Under The Window* (1878) was published in an edition of 20,000 copies which was disposed of so quickly that Edmund Evans, the printer, was unable to meet the demand. In the year of publication, some 70,000 copies were sold in Britain.

By the end of the 1880's there were large numbers of books available in most categories of fiction as is demonstrated by the following impressive classification of writers of boys' stories:

Adventure stories: R. M. Ballantyne, Harry Collingwood, G. M. Fenn, H. Rider Haggard, J. C. Hutcheson, W. H. G. Kingston, Captain Marryat, Mayne Reid, Gordon Stables and Robert Louis Stevenson.

Historical fiction: A. J. Church, James F. Cobb, J. G. Edgar, Percy Groves, G. A. Henty, Professor Hodgetts, and James Payn.

School stories: H. C. Adams, F. Anstey, Frederick Farrar, "Ascot R. Hope", Thomas Hughes, Rev. T. S. Millington, and Talbot Baines Reed.

Books for girls, however, were limited both in numbers and in variety of topics. It was far more difficult to interest readers in domestic affairs than in wars and other forms of adventure. Leading writers for girls were Mrs. Ewing, Mrs. Linnaeus Banks,

Anne Beale, Sarah Doudney, Emma Marshall, L. T. Meade, Adeline Sergeant, Anna Sewell, E. M. Sewell, and Charlotte M. Yonge, although the two latter had suffered some loss of popular esteem since their first success. Many of the stories at this time and earlier were *about* rather than *for* children, and were of more interest to adults than to those for whom they had been ostensibly written.

The 25 years after 1865 were prolific in books for younger children. Some male writers contributed with success, including Lord Brabourne (Knatchbull-Hugessen), Lewis Carroll, Tom Hood, Charles Kingsley, George MacDonald and Silas K. Hocking. The majority of writers for the very young were women, of whom the most prominent were Frances Havergal, Emma Marshall, L. T. Meade, Florence Montgomery, "Hesba Stretton", Charlotte Tucker, and Mrs. O. F. Walton. Probably the best storyteller in the history of children's literature was Mrs. Molesworth (Fig. 18), although Mrs. Ewing had outstanding qualities. In these years too the picture books of Crane, Caldecott and Greenaway were also popular.

It would be wrong to assume that all the children's books which had been published since 1744 were available in 1890. The chapbooks were not in use by 1840 and no editions of Newbery were issued in Victorian times. The most recent edition of Roscoe's *The Butterfly's Ball* was dated 1855, although an edition of his collected poems was published in 1891. No new editions had been produced since 1870 of Mrs. Barbauld's *Lessons for Children*, Maria Hack's *Winter Evenings*, or Agnes Strickland's *Rival Crusoes*. On the other hand it was possible to obtain new editions of *Evenings at Home*, *Sandford and Merton*, *The Parent's Assistant*, *The History of the Fairchild Family*, *The History of the Robins*, and *Tales of the Great and Brave*. Therefore, whilst some books made a continuous contribution to the growth of literacy, others made a relatively transient impact, and where they were not republished after 1870, their contribution was negligible to the cultural development of the working classes.

There were numerous editions for 19th-century children of

FIG. 18.   Title page from Mrs. Molesworth's *The Cuckoo Clock*.
1901 edition.

Aesop's *Fables* and *The Arabian Nights*, particularly after 1880. For most of the period, however, there was not a satisfactory edition of Perrault, whose stories appeared only in general selections of fairy tales. Unfortunately no edition was issued in the Victorian era of Sir Richard Phillips' *Popular Fairy Tales*, which included all Perrault's tales; and J. R. Planché's *Popular Fairy Tales* was not reissued after the edition of 1862. The first separate retelling of Perrault was that of Andrew Lang in 1888. In each decade of the 19th century, publication took place of numerous editions of the fairy tales of Andersen and Grimm.

During the 19th century, the work of an increasing number of continental writers became popular with British children. The earliest was Johann Wyss, whose *The Swiss Family Robinson* was a perennial favourite from Switzerland, and from the same country came Johanna Spyri's *Heidi*. Heinrich Hoffman's *Struwwelpeter* was translated from the German in the 1840's, and from Italy came Carlo Collodi's *Pinocchio* which was published in English by Unwin in 1891.

Probably the greatest European influence after 1870 was French. The science fiction stories of Jules Verne began to appear in England during the 1870's. These included *A Voyage to the Moon* and *Round the World in Eighty Days*. Verne underwent a good deal of criticism but his books were very popular with large numbers of boys.

The highly moral influence of children's books from the United States, typified by the work of Maria Cummins and Elizabeth Wetherell, grew less intense after 1865 in the domestic and adventure stories of Louisa M. Alcott, Mrs. Hodgson Burnett, Susan Coolidge, Martha Finley, and Mark Twain. Adventure stories in the tradition of Fenimore Cooper included work by Horatio Alger, Harry Castlemon, Elijah Kellogg, Oliver Optic, and J. T. Trowbridge. Fantasy was represented in the work of Joel Chandler Harris and Howard Pyle.

Books from the United States did not have a uniform popularity throughout the Victorian period. No editions of Jacob Abbott's works were produced in Britain after 1870, and even the phenomenal success of Samuel Goodrich was not maintained after 1880. On the other hand, numerous editions were available to the end of the century of the writings of most of the other authors.

International copyright between particular countries had been established on a reciprocity basis as a result of conventions after 1850. That between England and France took place in 1851. Agreements between nine countries were standardized by the Berne Convention of 1886. Whilst Wyss' *The Swiss Family Robinson* was never protected in this country, the copyright was respected in the cases of Collodi, Spyri, and Verne.

Until 1891, copyright in the United States was only obtainable by American citizens or residents in that country. Mrs. Ewing was informed by an American publisher that he was producing a cheap edition of *Jackanapes* (Fig. 19) and that he did not recognize the right of English writers "to control the market". In Britain the same practice persisted for many years, and as has been shown, many of the American books were very popular. If American writers were resident in Britain at the time their books were published then they were protected by British law. Authors frequently spent a day in Montreal when their books were published and thus became British subjects for the duration of their residence in Canada.

In a survey of children's reading made by Charles Welsh in 1884, it was found that the favourite authors of 790 boys aged 11 to 19 were Charles Dickens, Kingston, Scott, Marryat, Ballantyne, Ainsworth, Mayne Reid, Kingsley, Defoe, and J. G. Wood. Names which were not rated high in popularity were those of Farrar, Henty, "Ascot R. Hope", and Gordon Stables. Favourite titles were *Robinson Crusoe* and *The Pickwick Papers*, whilst the least favoured were Farrar's *Eric* and Marryat's *Masterman Ready*.

A similar survey among approximately 1000 girls in the same age group revealed a preference for Dickens, Scott, Kingsley, Yonge, Shakespeare, "Hesba Stretton", Mrs. Walton, Bunyan, and Emma Marshall.

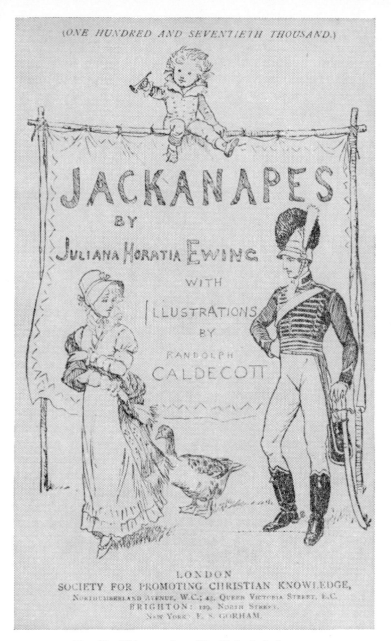

JACKANAPES

BY

JULIANA HORATIA EWING

WITH

ILLUSTRATIONS

BY

RANDOLPH CALDECOTT

LONDON
SOCIETY FOR PROMOTING CHRISTIAN KNOWLEDGE,
NORTHUMBERLAND AVENUE, W.C.; 43, QUEEN VICTORIA STREET, E.C.
BRIGHTON: 129, NORTH STREET.
NEW YORK: E. S. GORHAM.

FIG. 19. Title page from Mrs. Ewing's *Jackanapes*.

Editions of *The Swiss Family Robinson* and Verne's stories for boys enjoyed a continual popularity according to Welsh's survey, and the former was ranked second only to *Robinson Crusoe*. An apparently moderate popularity was enjoyed by Alcott, Fenimore Cooper, and Wetherell; and although the finding was understandable that boys entertained no enthusiasm for *Uncle Tom's Cabin*, much less accountable was their apparent distaste for Mark Twain.

The authenticity of surveys of that kind must always be considered in relation to the material which was available from which a choice could be made, and the presence or absence of pressure placed on a child to make a particular answer. Ainsworth, Dickens, Scott, and Shakespeare would not be regarded normally as writers for children, although their work was available in adapted editions. Edward Salmon, in commenting on Welsh's investigations, thought that the children made a choice which was "coloured by circumstances more or less accidental". He considered that support for Dickens and Scott did not represent a knowledge of their works but of their names, and that their books had probably been noticed in the school library without having been read. Salmon may have been correct in his analysis, and of course it is surprising that young people appeared to prefer adult books to their own literature. This is particularly true in the case of boys who had so much readable material at their disposal. The fact remains, however, that the children were aware of authors who had outstanding reputations in the field of English literature, and it is reasonable to assume that they profited from these writings.

Non-fiction works for children were still available in only small quantities. There were very few books of poetry apart from Robert Louis Stevenson's *A Child's Garden of Verses* (1885).

In science and natural history, Mrs. Gatty was a pioneering author and she published her authoritative *British Seaweeds* in 1862. She combined a high level of accuracy with non-scientific terminology. W. Houghton wrote *The Country Walks of a Naturalist with his Children* (1869) and *The Seaside Walks of a Naturalist with his Children* (1870). J. G. Wood continued to be popular with such works as *Lane and Field* (1879).

Other examples of non-fiction for children and young people were Mayne Reid's *Quadrupeds* (1867), Dr. G. Hartwig's *Subterranean World* (1871), and R. M. Ballantyne's *The Ocean and its Wonders* (1875). Dr. Scoffern wrote on electricity and chemistry, and Gordon Stables on dogs. The S.P.C.K. published popular history, science, and nature study, the quality of which rose remarkably from 1875, when Rev. Edward McClure became editorial secretary. He encouraged his friends who specialized in archaeological and scientific subjects to have their books produced by the Society.

In the last two decades of the century, various publishers issued series of books which dealt with non-fiction topics. Among these may be listed Allen's *Eminent Women*, Longman's *Epochs of Ancient History* and *Epochs of Modern History*, Macmillan's *English Men of Action* and *Twelve English Statesmen*, and Walter Scott's *Great Writers*. The principal difficulty is to distinguish non-fiction for recreational reading from the far more numerous literature designed for use in schools. It is possible to make a decision in cases where the terms *Educational*, *Readers*, or *School* were employed in series titles, but this is not an infallible guide.

The practice of binding children's books in cloth inlaid with gold became customary, and was adhered to until the 20th century in the form of either floral embellishment or an illustration from the story. Increasingly after 1860 the books were produced in octavo size although the publications of the R.T.S., for example the books of "Hesba Stretton", did not conform to this trend. The cloth-binding, however, was dominant, and when, in the 1870's, Walter Crane's picture books appeared in cardboard covers, they were regarded with hostility by the publishing trade. This "innovation" was necessary, however, if prices were to be kept within reasonable limits, as picture books were expensive to produce. The experiment was not apparently detrimental to sales.

Whilst boards were acceptable as an alternative to cloth, an increasingly discriminating public was antipathetic to paper covers. Mrs. Ewing's *Jackanapes* registered disappointing sales in its original stone-coloured paper covers. In order to achieve success the S.P.C.K. changed the binding from paper to cardboard on which was printed a coloured reproduction of the Union Jack, a shrewd recognition of the jingoistic spirit which prevailed at that time.

It was not until the 1860's that publishers first began to sell books for children principally for their illustrative content. Outstanding names were Arthur Hughes, the illustrator of stories by George MacDonald, and Sir John Tenniel, who was in this connection associated with Lewis Carroll. The Dalziel brothers were the leading engravers of the period, and for their successful edition of *The Arabian Nights* (1865) they commissioned work by A. B. Houghton, John Millais, George Pinwell, and Tenniel. The Dalziels introduced Lear to Routledge in 1861 and in so doing helped to immortalize his nonsense which had been as yet unrecognized.

The most prominent designer was Edmund Evans. Whilst he commissioned drawings he was unlike the Dalziels in that he normally engaged only one illustrator for a particular work. Among his discoveries were Crane, Caldecott, and Greenaway.

New children's books were obtainable at prices similar to those of 1830 to 1860. Kingsley's *The Water Babies* was 7s. 6d. (1863) but reduced to 5s. in 1871, and Carroll's *Alice* was 7s. 6d. (1865) but reduced to 6s. in 1869. Perhaps the outstanding development of the 1860's was the production of Crane's toy books at 6d. each.

In the 1870's and 1880's Mrs. Ewing's *The Brownies* (1870), George MacDonald's *At the Back of the North Wind* (1871), Crane's *The Baby's Opera* (1876), Greenaway's *Under the Window* (1879/80), Stevenson's *Treasure Island* (1883), L. T. Meade's *The Autocrat of the Nursery* (1884), and Andrew Lang's *Blue Fairy Book* (1889), all ranged in price from 5s. to 7s. 6d. The R.T.S. published its books at lower prices, and Mrs. Walton's *Little Faith* (1880) was 1s.

A few years after the original publication of books it was not unusual for their prices to be reduced. An edition of *At the Back of the North Wind* appeared in 1884 at 3*s. 6d.*, and one of *Alice* in 1887 at 2*s. 6d.* Numerous cheap series were produced and included Low's *Copyright Editions of American Authors* in 1871, all of which sold at 1*s. 6d.*, whilst the 1880's produced famous series which included Cassell's *Red Library* (1*s.*), Chambers's *Sixpenny Books for the Young*, Griffith & Farran's *Favourite Library* (1*s.*), Routledge's *Every Boy's Library* (paper covers 1*s.*, cloth covers 1*s. 6d.*) and Routledge's *Ruby Series* (6*d.*).

The prices of books in relation to the wages of the working people at this period show that most children could not afford to buy them, but might be able to obtain them on loan from school or public libraries, or receive them as prizes.

After 1870 the R.T.S. recognized the demand for prizes in the newly opened board schools. Most of the Society's best sellers were published in these years and included *Christy's Old Organ* (1873) and *A Peep behind the Scenes* (1878). The books were evangelistic in approach and were popular as Sunday school prizes. The houses of Nelson and Blackie also specialized in rewards. In 1882 the latter issued two books by G. A. Henty, *Facing Death* and *Under Drake's Flag*, and in so doing its commercial success was ensured. Other publishers became involved in the production of this class of literature, much of which presented no literary or aesthetic standards whatever, but provided young people with their own collections, and fostered the continued growth of literacy.

Children's periodicals were also a source of reading material which varied in quality, and may be grouped into the same categories as their books. They reflected also the pattern of development of periodical literature for adults.

During the 1820's the periodicals were of a religious character. They included *The Children's Friend* (1826–60), and *The Child's Companion* (1824 to the 20th century), the latter being sponsored by the R.T.S. After 1850 outstanding productions included *The Monthly Packet* (1851–98), which represented the tractarian view, and was intended to make girls "more steadfast and dutiful daughters of our own beloved Catholic Church of England";

Chatterbox (1866 to the 20th century) was designed to counteract the influence of some of the boys' papers then in vogue and was extremely pious; and *Good Words for the Young* (1868–77) cost 6*d.* and maintained a distinctive Christian outlook. In 1879 the R.T.S. published *The Boy's Own Paper* which upheld a religious tone of less intensity than *The Child's Companion*, and this was followed in 1880 by *The Girl's Own Paper*. The majority of children's periodicals were the products of religious organizations.

Peter Parley's *Children's Magazine of General Knowledge* (1842–71) reflected the contemporary interest in "useful knowledge". A similar publication was called *The Tiny Library* (1846). No attempt was made to convey the information in a palatable form.

As stories for boys became popular, so periodicals in the same category became available. *The Boy's Own Magazine* (1855–74) achieved a circulation of 40,000 copies per month in 1863, when the price was raised from 2*d.* to 6*d.* The publisher introduced *The Boy's Penny Magazine* for poorer children. *Boys of England* (1866–99) reflected jingoistic attitudes and at the cost of 1*d.* aimed to enthral its readers "by wild and wonderful but healthy fiction".

Girls were catered for by *Aunt Judy's Magazine* (1866–85) which was edited by Mrs. Gatty and latterly by her daughter Mrs. Ewing. Parents were assured that they "need not fear an overflowing of mere amusement".

For young children *Charm* (1852–4) had a brief existence which may be attributed to its failure to reflect public opinion in the 1850's. It was intended to offset the influence of religious periodicals and contained fairy tales and adventure stories. In 1871, Cassell's issued their highly successful *Little Folks*.

Between 1870 and 1914 a large number of periodicals were placed on the market. Many children did not visit bookshops or libraries, but were able to obtain periodicals for a few pence from bookstalls. During that period children's periodicals exerted an important influence on the growth of literacy.

It was the practice for children's stories to be serialized in periodicals prior to their publication in book form. This increased the accessibility of good quality stories to poorer children. The first stories of Mrs. Ewing were published in *The Monthly Packet* but most of her writings appeared in the pages of *Aunt Judy's Magazine*. Her contributions included *Mrs. Overtheway's Remembrances* (1866/7), *The Land of the Lost Toys* (1869), *Timothy's Shoes* (1871), *Six to Sixteen* (1872), and *Daddy Darwin's Dovecot* (1881). Many of Charlotte M. Yonge's stories were printed first in *The Monthly Packet*. In 1851 appeared *The Little Duke*, followed by *The Daisy Chain* (1853/6), and *The Trial* (1862/4). Talbot Baines Reed was a regular contributor to *The Boy's Own Paper* from its inception in 1879 until his death in 1893. Most of his school stories were printed in that periodical, including *The Adventures of a Three Guinea Watch* and *The Fifth Form at St. Dominic's*. Other contributors to *B.O.P.* were Henty, Kingston, Ballantyne, "Ascot R. Hope", and Verne. Writers for *Good Words For The Young* in 1869 included Mrs. Craik, and George MacDonald; whilst early contributors to *Little Folks* were Mrs. Ewing, and Kingston. The latter was associated also with *The Boys' Own Magazine*; and in 1880 founded the jingoistic *Union Jack* in the production of which he was succeeded by Henty.

Unfortunately, many authors had their work published in more expensive standard contemporary journals, rather than in children's periodicals. Kingsley's *The Water Babies* was serialized in *Macmillan's Magazine* (1862/3); Kipling's *Stalky and Co.* was published in *The Windsor Magazine* (1898); and E. Nesbit's Bastables were featured in *The Illustrated London News* (1897), whilst others were serialized in *The Strand Magazine*. All were reputable periodicals but none was a publication which was likely to be easily available to poorer children unless it could be seen in the public library.

The literature which has been described contributed in varying degrees to the literacy of children in Victorian England, and to other aspects of their development. For most of the period there were examples available of material to satisfy the needs of all age groups from childhood to adolescence, and this literature increased rapidly after 1860. Frequently, books not especially written for children were found to be suitable to their requirements. There was, however, a particularly large class of material which was easily accessible, which cost very little, and which not only contained subject matter unsuitable for children, but was also defective in its use of English.

Many of the "penny fiction" books were relatively innocuous, and contained a combination of melodrama and domestic sentiment. The sentences of which the stories were formed were short and unrhythmical in numerous instances, whilst in others they were extended into long and meaningless dialogues and descriptions. Their subject matter exhibited a depressing uniformity, and typical examples consisted of a few tales, columns of recipes, advertisements, and answers to correspondents.

In the 1880's "penny fiction" of the kind described began to be difficult to obtain in its serial form, but was still available in 6d. volumes, and was widely circulated among young people. Among the more unsuitable titles were *The Mysteries of the Court, The Mysteries of London, Maria Marten; or, the Murder in the Red Barn, Spring-heeled Jack; or, the terror of London,* and *Sweeney Todd: the demon barber of Fleet Street.*

In contrast to this type of publication, there were numerous periodicals in which were serialized the Bible, the history of England, and even editions of the works of Bunyan, Cervantes, Scott, Shakespeare, and other writers. Books of an educational character were published in serial form too, for example Cassell's *Popular Educator*, which at the cost of 1d. per issue was first issued in 1852. Cassell was estimated to have sold between 25 and 30 million copies of his penny publications each year in the 1860's, all of which contributed to the rapidly growing taste for reading. Other publishers emulated Cassell with cheap "libraries"; and in the years between 1880 and 1900, the development of the "penny dreadful" trade was counterbalanced by the availability of good quality works of fiction at comparable prices.

The factors which rendered "penny dreadfuls" detrimental to the growth of literacy in working-class children were the absence of correct English usage and a limited vocabulary. Some of the children's periodicals were open to criticism in this respect, for example, the stories in *Boys of England* were comprised of short, jerky sentences, and neither colons nor semi-colons were used in punctuation. It is true that the contents were frequently not helpful to a healthy development of personality in children, but in the present study, this factor must be regarded as of secondary importance.

CHAPTER 9

Elementary Education For All
1870–1902

THE Parliamentary Reform Act of 1867 had extended the franchise to the working people in the urban areas and it was necessary to educate them if they were to respond satisfactorily to their new privileges and responsibilities. Sir Lyon Playfair in an address to the Social Science Association in 1870 stated that

> You cannot give political power to a people and allow them to remain ignorant . . . They cannot grasp the ideas of the age in which they live and are powerless to shake themselves free from the prejudices which the progress of thought has proved to be dangerous errors. They are unable to do so as they cannot take possession of the inheritance of intellectual wealth accumulated by their predecessors: for they do not know how to read the books forming the testament by which it was bequeathed.

In 1870 it was estimated that only 40% of the working-class children aged 6 to 10 years, and only 33% of those aged 10 to 12, were at school. The Education Act of 1870 provided for the formation of School Boards in every school district which did not possess adequate facilities, and empowered them to formulate by-laws which would render compulsory the attendance at school of children aged 5 to 13. The London School Board implemented these provisions but granted exemption to children over 10 who had passed standard V, and who were obliged to work for domestic reasons. School boards in large towns followed a similar policy, but in country districts boards were often not established for many years and progress was slow. The urgency to educate inhabitants of rural communities did not exist until 1884 when agricultural labourers were enfranchised for the first time.

The 1870 Act allowed voluntary bodies 6 months in which to remedy any deficiencies which existed in their educational provision. The Societies were stimulated to build new schools, and between 1870 and 1880, 1 million new school places were made available. Whilst school boards received income from local rates, government grants, and fees, that of voluntary schools was confined to government grants, fees, and voluntary subscriptions. Government grants to voluntary schools were increased by the Education Act of 1876.

Successive legislation was intended to ensure the attendance of children at school. The Sandon Act of 1876 rendered parents liable to financial penalties if their children did not receive the required quantity of instruction, and the Mundella Act of 1880 stipulated that the framing of attendance by-laws should be compulsory. In 1882 compulsion was in operation throughout the country.

The Act of 1876 forbade the employment of children under 10 years of age, and those between 10 and 13 could only be employed if they achieved a prescribed standard of education or attendance. The Factory and Workshop Act of 1878 still permitted half-time employment in factories of children aged between 10 and 14, regardless of local by-laws, but the Mundella Act was interpreted as over-ruling the terms of the Factory Act, with the exception of children who were actually employed in 1880.

The number of half-timers fell from 201,284 in 1876 to 168,543 in 1886. Lancashire included more children in this category than the combined totals in all other counties. Very few half-timers were to be found in Liverpool and Manchester, but in the adjacent factory towns, schools in which they were not included were the exception. At Blackburn there were approximately 6000 children at school aged 10 to 13 of whom more than 5200 attended on a part-time basis, and they were frequently dull and overtired after their manual exertions.

In his preface to *Social Problems* (1873), Sir James Kay-Shuttleworth summarized the factors which had contributed to the gradual development of elementary education:

> The nation had to be awakened to a sense of its necessity; the religious communions had to be reconciled to the interference of the secular power; the school managers had to be trained in all the details of the

organization and discipline of schools; a numerous staff of teachers and assistant teachers had to be educated; and the local civic authority had to be prepared to vote the school rate.

There were 200 ragged schools in London in 1870 which were attended by 23,000 pupils, but most of the schools disappeared after the establishment of the school boards. Transfers became frequent in 1872 and 1873, and by October of the latter year, the London Board had accepted responsibility for 71 such schools, accommodating 53,082 children.

Unfortunately large numbers of dames' schools were not assimilated into the new system. In 1878 there were still hundreds of children in Leicestershire who were taught in unsuitable premises in these schools. Inspectors did not have the power to intervene and local authorities were often unwilling to do so. One inspector of schools in Yorkshire advocated that either they should be abolished or made subject to inspection.

As part of the extension of literacy an interest grew in the education of blind and deaf children. Attempts were made in London to induce blind children to attend ordinary schools in 1874, and in that year a class for the education of deaf children was commenced by the Board. In 1879 centres were organized for the instruction of blind children and books and apparatus were provided. A Royal Commission was appointed in 1885 to consider the education of the blind and the deaf. In its report in 1889 the Commission recommended that the education of the blind should be placed under government control, and that the age of compulsory instruction for these children should be raised to 16 years. The National Library for the Blind was founded in 1882, an example of voluntary enterprise which offered a complementary service to the educational developments.

However, the educational system as it existed was subjected to severe criticism. The large sums of money which were expended did not yield permanent results because the majority of children did not continue their education on leaving school. In 1886 almost 500,000 children left school at 12 or 13, but only 5% pursued their education beyond the elementary stage.

It was the intention of the London School Board to establish evening schools concurrently with day schools, but after an unsuccessful experiment in 1873, the Board did not commence its work in this sector until 1882. Representatives of the London Trades' Council, inspired by a scheme of recreative evening schools in Nottingham, proposed a similar plan to the School Board, which was duly accepted. However, there was a distinct loss of support for evening schools at a national level during the 1880's due to the extension of elementary education which rendered them less essential. Reports of inspectors from all parts of the country confirm this conclusion.

The Cross Commission on *The Elementary Education Acts* (1887) considered that the presence of evening schools was important, but recommended that they should be concerned with a continuation of education rather than with elementary instruction. Opportunities should be available for recreative activities and also for instruction in art, science and technology.

There was an immediate need for a closer integration of the educational system in England and Wales if its organization was to be efficient. The Bryce Commission on *Secondary Education* which reported in 1895 advocated "one properly constituted and organized central authority, sufficiently strong and enlightened to secure the effective and intelligent supervision of local bodies and institutions taking part in secondary instruction". In 1899 an Act of Parliament provided for the amalgamation of the three principal central authorities entrusted with the oversight of elementary, secondary, and technical education, and in the following year a Board of Education was formally constituted.

In 1902 an Education Act was passed which was probably the most important event in the history of education in England since the full recognition of elementary education as a national necessity in 1870. School boards were replaced by Local Education Authorities, which made possible a closer co-ordination of elementary and secondary education.

During the last decade of the 19th century the school leaving age was raised on three occasions. In 1893 the minimum age for exemption from school attendance, whether total or partial, was raised from 10 to 11, and the employment of children under 11 was prohibited. An Act of 1899 relating to attendance raised the age from 11 to 12 although under certain conditions children employed in agriculture could be partially exempted at the age of 11. Finally the Elementary Education Act of 1900 enabled school authorities to extend their by-laws to include children up to the age of 14.

The practice of half-time instruction was continued during the 1890's. 80·7% of the children were to be found in Lancashire and Yorkshire in 1895, whilst the remainder were distributed in small numbers throughout the country. The total decreased from 201,284 in 1876 to 126,896 in 1895, and to 77,426 in 1902.

Between 1870 and 1895 the numbers of scholars on the registers of day schools rose from 1,802,419 to 5,299,469; the numbers in average attendance rose from 1,231,434 (68·32%) to 4,325,030 (81·61%). In 1895 there were 7347 pupils in elementary schools over 15 years of age. In 1870 the average length of school life was 2·55 years; in 1880 it was 5·19 years; in 1890, 6·13 years; and in 1897, 7·05 years. Thus since 1870 the period actually spent in elementary schools in England and Wales by the average pupil was almost trebled.

Secondary education was also expanded. A scheme for Wales was effected through the Welsh Intermediate Education Act of 1889, although the first school was not opened until 1896. Intermediate education was defined as a course of instruction which included not only the three R's but also English language and literature, modern languages, Greek, Latin, and Welsh, mathematics, and natural and applied science.

Some school boards and voluntary bodies in England had introduced an extra standard; and others had founded "higher grade elementary" schools, which in fact were secondary in character, in order to cater for the increasing number of children who were staying at school for a longer period. By 1894, 17 secondary schools had been founded or were being founded by county councils in collaboration with the charity commissioners, governing bodies of endowed schools, or school boards. Forty-two out of forty-eight counties were spending part of their funds on scholarships, the majority of which were for children from public elementary schools between the ages of 11 and 14. In contrast, county boroughs had undertaken very little activity of this kind, and in 1893/4 only 14 out of 61 had made grants to secondary schools. Only 15 county boroughs had founded scholarships, but a large proportion of these were allocated to children from elementary schools. In 1895 only 2500 local authority scholarships were available to children from these schools. As has been shown, the Balfour Education Act of 1902 made possible a system of secondary education in England.

Opportunities for further education, as recommended by the Cross Report (1888), were realized by the Evening Continuation Schools Code of 1893. In anticipation of the Code numerous authorities such as Bradford organized evening schools for further education, and in 1894, 20 boroughs were allocating grants to school boards for the maintenance of these schools, in which the study of scientific and technical subjects was encouraged. In 1897 the evening schools included 358,628 students under the age of 21, the largest single group being 14 to 16; and by 1900 the attendance figures were six times as great as in 1892.

In the 1890's therefore, working-class children could either remain at day school engaged in subjects of a secondary character until they were 18, provided they attained success in the limited number of scholarships which were available; or continue their education at evening classes. In practice, however, large numbers of parents were unable to take advantage of the secondary school facilities, for due to their poor economic condition they required their children to work as soon as they reached the compulsory school leaving age. Intelligent children frequently won scholarships but were unable to profit from them. Even when they actually commenced their studies at secondary school there was no guarantee that they would remain there for a period which would be permanently beneficial to them, and many left at 14.

The education of backward children received official recognition after 1890. Children who were only mildly afflicted had usually attended ordinary elementary schools where they comprised the dullest group of pupils, but the worst cases remained at home. An Act of 1893 empowered school boards to provide for the education of blind and deaf children. This Act raised the age of compulsory attendance of blind and deaf children to 16 years, and partial exemption was not permitted. In 1899 another Act enabled School Boards to provide special accommodation for defective children.

CHAPTER 10

School Books and Literacy
1870–1902

IN 1870 the most expected of working-class children by the Government was that they should read a newspaper on leaving standard VI, a requirement which could well have been met by a child of 8 years old. Inspectors admitted that no attainment below standard IV could be of permanent benefit to a child, and yet 80% of children passed only in the lower standards before leaving school. Fewer than 10% of the children attended school for 4 years.

However, in the Code of 1871 the six standards were modified and a higher degree of attainment became necessary. Standard I was removed, the remaining five were renumbered and a new standard VI was added. Further improvements were effected in the Codes of 1881 and 1882 as follows:

Code of 1881: *Requirements in reading*

Standard
I	Read a short paragraph from a book not confined to words of one syllable
II	Read a short paragraph from an elementary reading book
III	Read a short paragraph from a more advanced reading book
IV	Read a few lines of prose or poetry selected by an inspector
V	Improved reading
VI	Improved reading

Intelligence and fluency were expected to increase after standard I. Reading was tested in the ordinary class books if approved by the inspector, but these books were to be of reasonable length and difficulty, and unmarked. Every class was to possess two or three sets of reading books although this was considered by many to be quite inadequate.

Code of 1882:   *Requirements in reading*

Standard
I   Read a short paragraph from a book not confined to words of one syllable
II   Read a short paragraph from an elementary reading book
III Read a passage from a more advanced reading book, or from stories from English history
IV   Read a few lines from a reading book, or history of England
V   Read a passage from some standard author, or from a history of England
VI   Read a passage from one of Shakespeare's historical plays or from some other standard author, or from a history of England
VII Read a passage from Shakespeare or Milton, or from some other standard author, or from a history of England

This schedule proves beyond a doubt that Edward Salmon was incorrect in his assumption that children would not be familiar with the leading exponents of English literature, and it is therefore possible to suggest that not only would children know such works, but in the hands of a good teacher, they would also enjoy them.

Reading with intelligence was now required in all the standards together with increased fluency and expression in successive years. Standard VII was introduced because children were remaining in attendance at school for a longer period. In this way the level of literacy was raised and its definition changed accordingly, so that in the parliamentary election of 1886, only 38,547 illiterates voted in England and Wales in a total poll of 2,416,272. Continuous improvement was shown in examinations, and whilst in 1872 children in standards IV to VI comprised only 17·96% of the school population, in 1886 the proportion had risen to 34·68%. Also, the index of backwardness diminished so that the proportion of scholars aged 10 and over presented in the lowest standards for examination purposes fell from 63·71% in 1872 to 36·33% in 1886.

Educationists were becoming increasingly aware that instruction in the rudiments of three subjects was insufficient for working-class children. Professor Laurie, who occupied the chair in

Education at the University of Edinburgh, called for the institution of a system which would develop in children the nobler feelings of human nature: love, tenderness, sympathy, a desire for approval, and a spirit of sacrifice. The syllabus was widened to include literature as an examination subject in 1871, and Matthew Arnold noted in his report for that year that the knowledge of this subject was "the greatest power available in education". In 1875 "class subjects" were introduced as a means of liberalizing the curriculum in the lower standards, and consisted of geography, grammar, history, and plain needlework; and in the early 1870's special grants were paid for passes in not more than two specific subjects by children in the upper standards. Thus in the upper school it became increasingly the custom to teach algebra, geometry, natural science, physical geography, political economy, and even French, German, and Latin. The list of "class subjects" was extended in 1880 to include any others "which can be reasonably accepted as special branches of elementary instruction and properly treated in reading books".

The terms of the Forster Act of 1870 resulted in a vast increase in the publication of school books, although the extent to which it would be necessary to reorganize their activities was not immediately apparent to many publishers. In 1875 William Collins II purchased the Scottish School Book Association for which he had been agent, for in the face of expansion the existing arrangements became unwieldy. 920 school books were listed in the catalogue for 1875 compared with 571 10 years earlier. Additional printing equipment was installed at Collins' in 1875 and in 1884, and innumerable other publishers were engaged in similar projects.

In 1879 Blackie's *Comprehensive Readers* were the first of what was to be a wide selection of school books in arithmetic, geography, grammar, and history. School editions of the classics were issued in the same year. Other publishers who were involved in the publication of school books were Bell, Blackwood, Cassell, Chambers, Constable, Gleig, Lockwood, Longman, Macmillan, Nelson, Rivington, Seeley, and Warne. Some of the firms produced more than one series of readers such as Blackie's *Advanced Readers*, *Elementary Text Books*, and *School Series*; Cassell's *Modern School Readers* and *School Board Series*, and Chambers's *Educational Course* and *English Readers*. Each publisher was not necessarily issuing new books continually, for example, no works in Gleig's *School Series* were published between 1872 and 1880. Inspectors expressed particular satisfaction with Bell's *Readers*, and Nelson's *Royal School Readers*, the latter of which were "more extensively used than any others" in many areas.

The contemporary opinion of reading books among progressive educationists was that attention to style was more important than the inclusion of a large amount of information. In a *Circular to H.M. Inspectors with Reference to the Approval of Schemes for Teaching Class Subjects* in 1881, the Committee of Council advocated the introduction of "a larger and fuller text book, attractive both in form and matter to young children". In 1884 the *Revised Instructions* to H.M.I.s referred to the length of lessons in books:

> It may be taken as a general rule that 40 lessons and not less than 80 pages of small octavo text should be required in standards I and II, and not less than 60 lessons and 120 pages in higher standards.

The purpose of this regulation was to prevent the use of books in which the contents were so meagre that they could be learned by heart in the course of a year, and represented no accurate test of a child's reading ability. Two pages were regarded as a minimum for an effective reading lesson and longer lessons were desirable for older children. Narratives and poetry could well be longer than those which dealt with technical information relating to geography, history and science.

During the two decades after 1870 a growing distinction was made between reading books and textbooks, a point which was stressed in the Circular to Inspectors in 1881. The reading books were intended to overcome mechanical difficulties in the lower standards and to present literary variety in the upper school. In addition to the two sets of books required for teaching reading, another set should be adopted for each separate subject; although in the higher standards the subject books would be of sufficient literary quality to be available for both purposes. This distinction between reading books and textbooks was not generally acknowledged immediately, and in 1888 an inspector remarked that many of the geographical readers contained "too many hard names to be good for instruction in reading".

Books on arithmetic, geography, and grammar were numerous and varied, and many new textbooks were continually being published. The Committee of Council felt that suitable geography books should include accounts of travels and descriptions of foreign countries and customs. Barrington-Ward's *The Child's Geography* was regarded as a successful attempt to obviate some of the difficulties and was found to be of considerable help in schools. Series were published by Gill (*Geographical Readers*), Longman (*New Geographical Reading Books*) and Macmillan (*Geographical Series*).

Ideally history textbooks should have concentrated on biographies and descriptions of life through the ages, which could be contrasted with the present. In practice there were very few such books, a factor which resulted in the frequent absence of history from the school curriculum. Existing works were excessively factual and style was sacrificed to the need for condensation. In the middle years of the 1880's historical readers were introduced into standards III to VII. They were very popular amongst children who became aware of events which some years earlier would have been unknown to their predecessors. Mandell Creighton's *Epochs of English History* for older children, was an outstanding series of its kind, as were the Longman series of *Epochs of Ancient History*, *Epochs of Modern History*, and *Highways of History*. Chambers's *Historical Readers*, the *English History Reading Book* of the National Society, and Nelson's *Pictures from English History*, were also available at that time.

A great deal of dissatisfaction was evidenced among inspectors and other educationists regarding the content of school books. One critic referred to "the scissor and paste compilations" and "ill-concealed sermonettes" of which many books were comprised. Reading books in elementary schools were the sole literature of many working-class children except where school and public libraries had been established, and there should have been no difficulty in superseding or supplementing the arid teachings of school books with materials from the rich sources of English literature. At first the call for good literature was unheeded but in the late 1880's the more progressive schools were adopting the proposal. Among standard works of literature suggested for use in schools were suitably adapted editions or the original texts of Carroll's *Alice in Wonderland*, Defoe's *Robinson Crusoe*, Hughes' *Tom Brown's School Days*, Scott's novels such as *Kenilworth*, essays by Macaulay, and plays by Shakespeare. Non-fiction works which were commended included Mrs. Brassey's *The Voyage of the Sunbeam*, Jevons' *Primer of Political Economy*, Scott's *Tales of a Grandfather*, and Southey's *Life of Nelson*. An enterprising inspector recommended that toy books or little story books should be provided for use by children in infants' schools.

The attitude to books during this period however was not wholly favourable, and opposition was probably crystallized as a result of the long-term economic depression between 1874 and 1896. It became evident that technical instruction was necessary to national prosperity and this was furthered in the report of the Devonshire Commission on *Scientific Instruction* in 1875, the establishment of the City and Guilds Institute in 1880, the re-organization of the South Kensington Science and Mines' Schools in 1881, and the Technical Instruction Act in 1889.

Mundella's Code of 1882 encouraged the teaching of elementary science, a subject for which it was widely agreed, books were accessories rather than principals. The London School Board approved the provision of textbooks in arithmetic, geography, and grammar, but all other subjects were to be taught orally. After 1890 elementary science grew in popularity along with other subjects of a practical character.

Fitch admitted that for a teacher to impart rudimentary facts which could be read in a textbook was a dissipation of teaching power, and it was for this reason that books were made available in science. Among the numerous series published in scientific subjects were Cassell's *Scientific Manuals*, Chambers's *Elementary Science Manuals*, Gill's *Albany Elementary Science Readers*, and Macmillan's *Science Class Books*.

The Committee of Council was adamant that inspectors must not recommend the use in schools of any particular books, but it was widely held that managers and teachers required guidance in their selection. It has been shown that in practice the Committee maintained some control over the publication of school books in the Instructions to Inspectors, and in 1884 the latter were permitted to "disallow the use of any books which are plainly unsuitable, or which do not conform to the requirements of the Code".

A further controlling factor in the use of school books was the appointment of school boards after 1870, in which many of the members were highly qualified to exercise supervision. The London School Board found it necessary to withdraw numerous books from schools under its control because they infringed the rules which related to religious instruction. A recommendation that the Board should issue textbooks of its own was rejected but a list of readers was compiled. An agent was appointed to supply and deliver items required by schools at a standard rate of discount, but in order to effect economy in dealings with manufacturers and publishers, a Central Store was established by the Board in 1874.

The appointment of school boards, which enjoyed such wide powers and an availability of adequate finance, was instrumental in securing higher standards of provision in schools. The effect of the reforms was detrimental to the voluntary schools for which the burden became so overwhelming that many of them opted to be placed under the jurisdiction of the new boards.

The report of the Cross Commissioners in 1888 represented a watershed in the attitude to books in schools. It was claimed that no case had been established for the prescription and recommendation by inspectors of particular books, and it was stressed that if inspectors wrote books themselves then their names must not appear upon the title pages. The Commission was opposed to the introduction of a set of government approved textbooks but considered it useful to publish an extended curricular programme so that managers and teachers would be increasingly aware of the requirements of the syllabus and select their books accordingly. There was a need to increase the number of books to be read in school to develop in children a taste for reading because

> . . . a child who has thoroughly acquired the art of reading with ease has within its reach the key of all knowledge, and it will rest with itself alone to determine the limits of its progress.

This statement marked a significant development in the official attitude to the growth of literacy in the working classes towards the close of the 19th century.

There was little relationship, however, between the standards of working-class literacy as envisaged by the Cross Commissioners and the situation as it existed in the schools, and whilst there was a high degree of fluency there was insufficient evidence of under-standing. Standards in reading varied from one school to another more than in any other subject of the curriculum, but "on the whole" there was evidence of progress.

Revised Instructions were issued to inspectors in 1896. It was stipulated that at least two reading books, each of which must contain at least 80 pages of small octavo text, were required for standards I and II. For upper standards at least three books were required in which the minimum number of pages was 120. School books were to be written in good English, attractive in style, and interesting in content. Fairy tales, fables and anecdotes of animals were recommended for younger children; whilst for older children narratives and poetical and literary extracts were considered to be appropriate. Lessons should illustrate the importance of thrift, temperance, good conduct as a means to well-being and success, gentleness, consideration for others, and kindness to animals.

The attitude was increasingly held that children should find pleasure in their school books and should also know how to locate any information which they required. In view of this it was imperative that the character of school books should be the subject of close scrutiny by the publishers who produced them, the managers who purchased them, and the teachers who used them.

Jarrold the publisher issued a set of *Empire Readers* which were adopted by the London School Board and met most of the suggestions made by inspectors. The series reduced the difficulties of beginners to a minimum by the use of large clear type, and by confining the attention to words of similar sounds and combinations of letters in the books for younger children. A careful graduation of lessons ensured continuous progress, and a large number of dialogues served to produce natural and easy reading in place of monotonous chanting. Particular attention was given to the inclusion of lessons which were interesting and within the range of children's comprehension, whilst at the same time using work from recognized authors.

Collins was responsible for the innovation of coloured illustrations in school readers in which half-tone blocks were overprinted lithographically in colour to resemble colour drawing. From 1891 for many years this method was used with great success in their *Graphic School Books* which sold in hundreds of thousands. Later, a series of *New Graphic Readers* was published and the books were the first of their kind to be illustrated with pictures in three colours. At the request of the London County Council, Collins designed *The Wide World Readers* which included reproductions of historical paintings from British and European art galleries. This latter series was produced in a quarto format which was a complete departure from the traditional octavo and duodecimo sizes of school books.

The 1890's were years of tremendous output both at elementary and latterly at the secondary school level. Arnold-Forster's *History of England from the Landing of Julius Caesar to the Present Day*, published by Cassell in 1897, enjoyed sales of 50,000 copies. His *Our Great City; or London the Heart of the Empire* (1900) was similarly successful. Unfortunately there were few outstanding histories of England for children in elementary schools, and the majority were arid epitomes. The content of these books was devoted to ecclesiastical disputes, military operations and party politics.

Geography books all too often contained the names of places which were devoid of either interest or importance to children. Some were encyclopaedic and overwhelming in factual detail.

Among a vast number of series at this time may be mentioned Bell's *History Readers*, Black's *School Geography*, Black's *School Shakespeare*, Blackie's *Raleigh Geography Readers*, Blackie's *Raleigh History Readers*, Longman's *Sullivan School Series*, Methuen's *Science Primers*, Nelson's *Royal Osborne Geography Readers*, Nelson's *Royal Windsor History Readers*, and Nelson's *Supplementary Readers*.

The expenditure of schools on books had grown to great proportions through Victoria's reign. Between 1839 and 1870, only £52,000 was spent on books and apparatus from a total expenditure of almost £12 million, and the following figures show the expenditure of elementary schools inspected for grants in the years 1880, 1890 and 1900:

	Books and apparatus	Total expenditure	Schools	Average no. pupils in attendance
1880	£311,860	£5,098,456	17,743	2,796,985
1890	£426,698	£7,566,964	19,568	3,761,264
1900	£874,754	£12,453,006	20,100	4,666,130

In 1880 the expenditure on books was 6·1% of the total, in 1890 it had decreased slightly to 5·5%, and in 1900 it had increased to 7%. A national movement towards a less bookish and more practical system of education during the depression from 1874 to 1896, threatened the progress which had been made in the use of books. However, the steady increase in the school population and the needs of other areas of the curriculum ensured that the attention given to books was not counterbalanced significantly. A scheme of education which was designed to meet the practical requirements of the working people would have been futile if the literacy of that increasingly influential section of the community was neglected.

CHAPTER 11

School Libraries
1870–1902

THE broader curriculum of the 1870's coincided with a revival of interest in school libraries. It cannot be known for certain whether or not the libraries formed between 1830 and 1850 survived the stagnancy of the following two decades. Certainly in 1870 many of the ragged schools in the country possessed lending libraries. Ninety-five such collections in London contained approximately 17,000 volumes, and children who had attended school for 6 weeks and were well behaved were allowed to borrow one book at a time for home reading. In cases of misconduct the privilege of using the library was withdrawn for a limited time.

Inspectors of schools increasingly attached importance to libraries. Particularly outspoken in this connection was D. P. Pennethorne, H.M.I. for Northumberland, who drew attention in 1876 to the lack of culture in the homes of poor children, and the unimaginative and mechanical teaching of reading at school. He urged the establishment of school lending libraries for the purposes of vocabulary building and for general culture, which should include "light entertaining books of travel, biographies of great men" and like material. Similar appeals were made by the inspectors of schools for Hull, Durham and Liskeard in 1880, Huddersfield and Liverpool in 1882, and Leeds in 1884.

The inspectors were not in agreement as to the inclusion of novels. Pennethorne was against the idea, whilst R. S. Stevelly of Hull advocated *Robinson Crusoe*, and the novels of Dickens, Fenimore Cooper, Marryat and Scott as a counterbalance to "trashy periodicals" and "records of the deeds of murderers and highwaymen".

Joshua Fitch, H.M.I., discoursed at some length on the value of libraries in schools and the kind of material which they should include, in his *Lectures on Teaching* (1881). He viewed them as a means of refining taste, increasing knowledge, and awakening a love of reading in children, and believed that once their enthusiasm had been aroused they and their parents would subscribe to the purchase of books, and kindly friends would donate material. Fitch recommended "books of reference"; a sufficient range of material to ensure that adequate use could be "made of the library for legitimate school purposes", and also for leisure and enjoyment. He wanted to include "the whole domain of wonderland, of fancy, of romance, of poetry, of dreams and fairy tales" which would not lead to knowledge in the narrow sense, but to "wisdom and insight and power". Books which Mr. Fitch would exclude were poorly written works in which the authors affected "childishness and simplicity", and all books which the teacher was sorry he had ever read, would be ashamed to be seen reading, or which he believed to be harmful to children.

A scheme of libraries was commenced by the London School Board in 1878. Schools were divided into groups of approximately 10,000 children at first, and each school's collection was changed after 6 months. It was found that the potential value of a collection to a school was not exhausted in 6 months, so in 1882 the system was amended, the groups abolished, and the period of retention extended to one year. There were 250 libraries in 1878 which had increased to 350 in 1887, each with a collection of 100 to 150 volumes. Only children in the upper standards were allowed library facilities and they were able to borrow books for home reading on a fortnightly basis. Teachers were encouraged to submit lists of popular books to the board, and these included not only the standard literature of Dickens, Macaulay, Shakespeare, Tennyson, and Thackeray but also boys' stories by Ballantyne, Henty, Kingston, and Marryat. By means of these libraries some 40,000 volumes of good literature were in constant circulation among the working classes of London.

Inspectors were able to report libraries in other parts of the country. Most of the board schools at St. Austell contained libraries provided by members of the board, and there were others in various parts of the Liskeard district in 1880. Some schools in Liverpool had started libraries with success, as had two of the largest schools in Leeds by 1884. In 1882 there were 1954 libraries in Anglican schools and this represented an increase of 131 on 1881. Rather more than 17% of the Church schools; 10% of the British, non-sectarian, Roman Catholic and board schools; and 6% of the Wesleyan schools possessed libraries in 1883.

The value of the school libraries depended to a large extent on the importance attached to them by teachers in individual schools. If a teacher was accustomed to using books in his work he was more likely to encourage his pupils to do so. During the 1880's a number of libraries were formed for the use of teachers, and there is evidence of such collections in London, Beccles, and Dewsbury. The school library movement spread through the 1880's and 1890's. In the *Minutes of Evidence* heard by the Cross Commissioners in 1887 there were reports of libraries in every board school in London, and there had been real progress in numerous towns in the provinces such as Bradford and Sheffield.

Some difficulty appeared to have arisen as regards the payment of grants. It was evident that financial aid was necessary, particularly in rural areas, if school libraries were to survive, and the Education Department had in fact sanctioned an outlay of grants by the school board in Sheffield. However, the Chairman of the Liverpool School Managers' Committee referred to rumours that the cost of a library could not be met from grants, but this did not emanate from the Education Department. The confusion arose from a recommendation by the Comptroller and Auditor General in his report to Parliament in 1887, when he suggested that the establishment of a store of books for reference or amusement "was not related to the purposes of elementary schools".

The Cross Commission reported in favour of libraries in schools and strongly advocated their establishment "as material encouragement to the habit of reading at home, and as forming important aids to the school course of teaching in securing a taste for reading". There were 4401 libraries in schools in 1890 as compared with 2092 in 1880 (the first year in which a record was kept), and 3589 in 1885.

In 1890 the Revised Instructions to H.M.I.s contained a request that an inquiry should be made into the use of libraries in schools. It was revealed that there were many such libraries at Hull, only 41 at Portsmouth where the collections ranged in size from 60 to 1000 volumes. The statistical evidence was encouraging in that in 1895, out of 19,709 schools inspected in England and Wales, 6225 included libraries. On the other hand, a percentage of 33% was hardly satisfactory, and inspectors' reports did not generally reflect optimism.

Many of the existing libraries catered for older children only, and it was felt that the younger children should also have facilities made available to them. There can be no doubt that where children had access to libraries the results were to their intellectual advantage. Public libraries were making some impact in towns in spite of the small rate which could be levied on their behalf, but the need was great in rural areas.

The Instructions to Inspectors were further revised in 1896, and the Committee of Council summarized the situation of libraries as being inadequate, and that even where they existed, they were not used satisfactorily. It was stated that "a good library may be considered as the necessary complement of an efficient school apparatus and should be proportioned to the number in average attendance". The main object of a school library was to teach children to regard books "as a never-failing source of pleasure and profit", so that they would be more likely to retain the reading habit after their formal education was completed.

The Committee of Council recommended that:

1. The library should be circulated among the class teachers who could ensure that the children read books suitable to their age and intelligence;
2. Girls should have the same library facilities as boys, and in larger schools, a separate collection made available in the girls' department;
3. The use of the public library should be encouraged and its facilities explained to the children by talks and visits;

4. A scheme of circulating libraries should be adopted by School Boards in towns, and by a combination of schools in country districts;
5. The National Home Reading Union, or a similar system may be a valuable teaching instrument in the upper Standards as a means of fostering both the continuation of reading throughout life, and a more intelligent comprehension of reading matter.

This was the first real evidence of the Government encouraging school libraries in general, although when Arthur Acland, M.P., Vice-President of the Committee of Council, opened the new Hermit Road Board School in March 1894, he remarked that he would like to see in every school a good library with books adapted to the intellect of children of all ages. He believed that all the best and most expensive picture books, and the best books which were found in the houses of the wealthy, should be available to the children in the board schools.

The Committee of Council reported an increasing interest in library provision in 1897. That year there were 7066 libraries in schools; in 1900 there were 8114, containing an average of 221 volumes in each; and in 1902 there were 8504.

A glowing account was given of managerial generosity at Newton Abbot, where a school was not only provided with a library for the children, but also with a good reference library for teachers. The occasion of Queen Victoria's Diamond Jubilee in 1897 provided the opportunity for raising a subscription from old pupils for a library of over 500 volumes at the boys' board school in the Denbighshire village of Penygelli.

It was possible for managers to apply for aid from the Education Department for the formation of libraries, but relatively few, if any, took advantage of the facilities. Many schools relied on public libraries to provide books for children. Until the public library organized collections at schools in Cardiff they "were regrettably rare". In many instances where they existed, the books were "often as dry as the covers were dusty". Many teachers had acquired pianos for their schools by means of entertainments, and several had raised funds for excursions, but they had not envisaged such activities as contributing to the provision of libraries.

Even when the Committee of Council and its successor, the

Board of Education, recommended the value of libraries in schools, their advocacy could only remain impotent whilst the teachers were not aware of the importance of books. A teacher's commitment to the cause of school libraries depended on his having had previous experience of books being used at home and at school, or enjoying a wide use of books during his period of training. There is little evidence to suggest that student teachers were accustomed to using books widely at college, and in cases where some attention was given to the subject, it would require a very intensive course to counterbalance the absence of books in childhood.

The use of books was not widespread in schools due to the method of teaching which was practised. It was the custom for classes to read by rote from copies of a single textbook, and little, if any, attention was given to children learning for themselves. In these circumstances a large collection of books for curricular purposes was an irrelevance, but it could be justified if the aim was to form good reading habits in children. Then, as now, the importance of a school library only increased in proportion to the amount of "active learning" which took place in a school.

It can be argued that public libraries functioned to provide reading facilities for children, and for this reason there was no necessity for schools to do so. However, at its most active, the public library only influenced children who were interested in reading. On the other hand, the school was concerned with the whole range of intelligences and preferences of children. It could guide more children each day of the week than would ever of their own volition use a public library.

A possible shortcoming of the school library was its inaccessibility at holiday times, but if, as suggested in the Instructions to Inspectors, children were encouraged to visit the public library, then the temporary closure of school need not deprive them of reading facilities.

The role of Sunday schools diminished in the secular field of education after 1850, but the authorities of these bodies considered that whilst their secular purpose ceased to exist, the religious aspects of their work actually increased after 1870. In districts where the only weekday education was supplied by board schools, free as they frequently were from religious content in their curriculum it was believed that there must be considerable re-organization in the Sunday school sphere, if the poor were not to be ignorant of the tenets of Christianity. The S.P.C.K. in 1874 offered financial assistance to clergy in the renting of board schools for the purposes of religious instruction on Sundays.

In the second half of the 19th century, Sunday schools continued to provide libraries, but many of the collections deteriorated and did not receive the repairs and replenishment which were required. Their importance gradually decreased as public libraries developed, although they remained influential in rural areas. In view of the provision of secular literature in both schools and public libraries, it is not surprising that Sunday school libraries at that time were mainly devoted to religious subjects.

A narrow view of children's reading requirements was reflected in the books which were available. Libraries in Lancashire and Cheshire were usually very small, the largest not consisting of more than 4000 volumes. Most of the books were not written for children, nor were they necessarily of interest to them. The library at the Peter Street schools in Manchester in 1879 was noted for its collection on the growth of Swedenborgianism in England.

Thomas Greenwood suggested that books should be included on elementary science, travel, history, natural history, and good quality fiction. He appreciated that the aim of Sunday school collections must be to foster "the moral and intellectual nature of the readers", which he did not consider to be often effected through books "in which the name of the Almighty appeared profusely on every page". A similar plea was made at the annual meeting of the Nottingham branch of the Sunday School Union in 1893.

There was a reason for the presence of so much pious literature in Sunday school libraries quite apart from the religious function of the schools. The principal sources from which books were obtained were the R.T.S., the Sunday School Union, and the S.P.C.K.

There had been less material of the kind criticized by Greenwood on the lists of the two former societies during the latter years of the century, and the S.P.C.K. had been responsible for books on a wide range of topics for many years. Unfortunately, due to insufficient funds, Sunday schools were frequently more concerned with quantity than quality in their selection of material either for prizes or for inclusion in libraries. It was normally possible to obtain books from booksellers at a discount of 25 % in these years of the "cheap book" movement, but Sunday school teachers were not always aware of this.

Reading circles were frequently organized with the assistance of the Victoria Reading Circle of the Sunday School Union, which aimed to recruit groups of young people for the purposes of self-culture. The National Home Reading Union, the value of which was endorsed by the Committee of Council in 1896, included a Young People's section. In the session of 1891/2 members were asked to read either individually or in groups, Hawthorne's *Tanglewood Tales*, Scott's *Marmion* and *The Talisman*, Dickens' *A Christmas Carol*, Longfellow's narrative poems, histories by Mandell Creighton and S. R. Gardiner, geography by A. Geikie, and some biography and "miscellaneous literature". Most of the titles suggest a preoccupation with instruction rather than with entertainment.

CHAPTER 12

Public Libraries for Children
1870–1902

THE real impetus to the growth of public libraries came after the passing of the Forster Education Act of 1870. Only 50 local authorities in the United Kingdom had adopted the Public Libraries Act at that date, but by 1898 there were 340 such districts, nearly 300 of them being situated in England and Wales, and in July 1900 the total had reached 401.

In addition to successive educational legislation, other factors contributed to the development of public libraries in the last three decades of the 19th century. The Library Association was founded in 1877, and from its inception an interest was taken in library work with children. There are numerous articles and news items to be found in the professional journals and reports of annual meetings between 1880 and 1902, which confirm this assertion. A Royal Charter was granted to the Association on 17 February 1898, and in this document its aims and objects were tabulated. The Association's function was "to unite *all* persons engaged or interested in library work", although at that time the vast majority of the members were in public libraries.

A further stimulus was the generous distribution, by Andrew Carnegie, of grants for the provision of free libraries, but this did not occur until the last decade of the century. 225 libraries were established in England and Wales between 1897 and 1913, due to the munificence of Carnegie. Unfortunately the grants were dissipated in many instances in the erection of palatial buildings, whilst the limitation of the rate allocation prevented the authorities concerned from providing adequate collections of books.

There were approximately 40 libraries throughout the country in 1891 which possessed special collections of books for children, and there was an increasing recognition of the need to extend library facilities of this kind wherever possible. In 1898 there were 108 public libraries in England and Wales which had made provision for young people, 36 of which publicized their work through teachers in the schools. Greenwood listed nearly 40 libraries in England and Wales which had separate children's rooms in 1900 in his *Library Year Book* for 1900/1901.

Notable examples of library work with young people after 1870 were at Cambridge from 1872, Manchester from 1878 (a revival of the earlier work in a time of economic depression), Plymouth from 1879, Newcastle upon Tyne from 1880, Nottingham from 1882, and Bootle from 1891 (Fig. 20).

The means by which the libraries were commenced was not uniform, and it would be wrong to assume that the expenditure which was incurred was met necessarily from the local rates. The approval by the library committee at Cambridge in 1871 of a children's library was given on the condition that expenses were not met from the rates. At Nottingham the children's library was established with a grant of £500 from Samuel Morley, M.P., a local manufacturer, and the library committee at Loughborough was able to provide facilities with the assistance of a grant of £50 from the trustees of a local charity. Thomas Greenwood referred to the generosity of J. Passmore Edwards, who had "done for Cornwall . . . what a niggardly legislative provision prevented communities from doing for themselves".

The principal obstruction to progress in public libraries was the small rate of 1*d.* in the pound which it was possible to levy on their behalf. There were various advocates of a scheme of government grants for the formation and support of this type of library, but no official approval could be obtained for such a proposal either in 1850 or when the legislation of the ensuing 40 years was consolidated and amended in the Public Libraries Act of 1892.

Whilst public libraries did not qualify for government grants, local authorities were permitted to promote legislation relating

BOROUGH OF BOOTLE

CATALOGUE

OF

BOOKS FOR THE YOUNG

IN THE

FREE PUBLIC LIBRARY.

———

COMPILED BY

CHARLES H. HUNT,
Librarian,

AND

WILLIAM T. MONTGOMERY,
Sub-Librarian.

———

FOURTH EDITION, REVISED & ENLARGED.

———

BOOTLE:
PUBLISHED AT THE FREE PUBLIC LIBRARY, ORIEL ROAD.
PRINTED AT THE "TIMES" OFFICE, MILLER'S BRIDGE.
———
APRIL, 1901.

FIG. 20.   Title page from the Bootle Public Library: *Catalogue of Books for the Young.* 1901 edition. (By courtesy of the Bootle Public Library.)

solely to their own localities. It was possible to include clauses which would empower them to raise the amount of rate which could be levied for library purposes. Local Acts were passed for Birmingham, Manchester, Oldham, and Cardiff, among other places. The public library rate at Cardiff was increased from $1d.$ to $1\frac{1}{2}d.$ in the pound under the terms of a local Act.

There was a large number of towns and villages throughout the country where there was no provision of public libraries at all. As late as 1896, 46 districts with populations in excess of 20,000 had refused to adopt the Public Libraries Act. John Ballinger, the librarian of Cardiff, deplored the absence of opportunities for children in many parts of the country to continue their reading after their school days were concluded.

Opposition to public libraries was particularly noticeable in London. In 1887 only two parishes in the whole of the metropolitan area had made library provision from the local rate. It may be assumed that the absence of facilities for children was due to the existence of the scheme of school libraries which had been sponsored by the London School Board since 1878, but it is difficult to explain the situation satisfactorily as it affected adults.

With the exception of Chelsea, there was no special library service for children in the West End of London in 1897. It was customary for boys to congregate at the Chelsea library on Sundays from Battersea, Fulham, and elsewhere. However, there was a gradual increase in library services in other parts of London. In the last decade of the century and in the early years of the 20th century, provision of varying standards was made in the north at Hampstead, Stoke Newington, Kilburn, and Tottenham; in the south at Camberwell, Bermondsey, and Lambeth; in the east at Clerkenwell, Whitechapel, and Bethnal Green; and in the west at Battersea and Hammersmith. At Camberwell and Bethnal Green, separate rooms were made available to children, but in most instances, they were expected to use the adult lending library.

Children's libraries were established at various locations. Most of them occupied separate rooms in the main library. Reading rooms for boys were provided in Manchester branch libraries, the first of which was at Ancoats in 1878. The children's library at Nottingham was situated in a separate building and was the first of its kind in Britain, but the librarian, Potter Briscoe, was explicit that he did not regard the facilities as ideal, and would have preferred to use part of his central library, had the accommodation there been adequate. A separate building was also rented at Reading.

It was important that the bookstocks in children's libraries should be selected on as systematic a basis as possible. Potter Briscoe's criteria were that the books should be related to the ages of the users, and that there should be a wide variety of material. He claimed to exclude school books, and the category known as "goody-goody" books "which disgust children of our day", and provided books which were "manly and robust". He extended his comments to the physical appearance of books, advocating the use of good quality paper, printing, and illustration, and stipulating that under no circumstances should works printed in type smaller than long primer be admitted. Thomas Greenwood was eager for the "penny dreadful" to be supplanted "by books of a stirring and exciting character" and suggested that the content should be "so simple that an untutored intellect can grasp it without effort". Butler Wood opted for books "which serve to gild the pill of instruction", and cited Courteney's *Travels in the Interior*, a work written to teach young people the elementary principles of human physiology. Wood claimed that the demand was growing for books on natural history, travels, and history, whilst ordinary children's books were in less request. This dichotomy of opinion represented the continuous struggle between the exponents of entertainment and didacticism which had persisted from the commencement of publishing and writing for children in the late 17th and early 18th centuries. The call for a large non-fiction content in libraries was also made by many librarians in order to ensure their association with education, a light in which they were not seen by the majority of people in those days.

Unfortunately the specially selected collections were frequently inadequate to meet the needs of their potential readers. At Cambridge approximately 600 books were collected between 1871 and 1873 and almost 300 readers were enrolled. Eight hundred entertaining books were provided for boys and girls in the juvenile section at Wigan in 1879. At Nottingham there were approximately 3500 children's books in 1890, "all carefully selected" and used by 2000 children; and in 1897, the Newcastle upon Tyne children's library contained 3500 volumes. The number of books listed in the Bootle Public Library *Catalogue of Books for the Young* increased enormously between 1891 and 1901, that is from 1173 to 2849. An analysis of the annual reports of 36 public libraries in 1891, showed that more than 50% had children's collections consisting of fewer than 1000 volumes.

There was no uniformity in the conditions by which children could become members of public libraries. In most cases both boys and girls were allowed access to the facilities, but in minor instances, as at Manchester and Chelsea, the service was restricted to boys. Many libraries had a minimum age limit ranging from 12 to 16 years.

Rules were framed to ensure the good behaviour of children and the responsible treatment by them of public property. At Bootle, the rules of the public library, which applied to adults, also applied, with certain exceptions, to children who lived in the borough. Parents and guardians were expected to act as guarantors before the children could be admitted to the library; and books could be borrowed only if they were included in the *Catalogue of Books for the Young*, a stipulation which was far from restrictive in view of the variety of its contents.

At Battersea the approval of parents was necessary before children could join the library; and at Nottingham, clean faces and hands were essential qualifications, in addition to parental consent. These rulings operated to the advantage of the middle- and respectable working-class children. It is open to conjecture how fared the "children of parents whose poverty draws them perilously near to the borderland of crime" but who were "still too young to have crossed that border themselves" (Credland).

In some libraries it was possible for children to use the adult lending department when they attained a stipulated age. At Stoke Newington the minimum age for membership was 10, and at Penge, 14. In view of the very slow growth in literacy among children in the late 19th century, it is not surprising that many librarians did not consider it necessary to extend adult facilities to the young. However, an increased number of children was able to read after 1870. Also, the tendency of children to remain at school longer coupled with the growth of secondary education in the closing years of the century, rendered it necessary for public libraries to lower the age limits, and so give access to those who could profit thereby. At Nottingham the minimum age limit had remained static at 14 years since 1867, but in 1900 it was reduced to 13. Similar relaxations were made at Chester (12 to 10), Hammersmith (13 to 11), and Kilburn (14 to 12). An additional advantage of this movement was that it enabled young people to retain their membership of the library, having exhausted their interest in children's books, and so facilitate a continuation of their reading habits as adults.

It was important that the appointment of librarians should be undertaken with care. Individuals were chosen frequently with no qualifications whatever for a career in librarianship, with very little educational background, and who had been "pitchforked into these positions by friends" (*Greenwood's Library Year Book*, 1897). Potter Briscoe recommended that children's librarians should possess the normal qualifications of library assistants, but should in addition have a liking for children and be accustomed to dealing with them.

The provision of books for young people was usually at its most successful where there was co-operation between public libraries and the schools. The first known instances of such co-operation were at Leeds in 1884 and at Plymouth in 1888. Whilst the rooms provided in schools were regarded as public

library branches, they were in fact intended for use by the children in attendance at the board schools.

Between 1885 and 1900 schemes of public-library–school co-operation were initiated in various parts of the country. Norwich provided libraries in elementary schools in 1889, and was followed by Birmingham and Leicester. The work begun by J. J. Ogle at Bootle in 1894 was particularly commendable. He modelled his scheme on one practised in Chicago, and was imitated in turn at Oldham and Barry. Interest was shown in Ogle's work at Bolton and Bristol. Similar schemes were in operation at Cardiff from 1898, and at Blackburn, Cambridge and Reading from 1900.

It would be erroneous to assume that in all cases books were provided where none had previously existed. There were already school libraries at Leeds and Plymouth. The Bootle School Board had established small lending libraries in each of its two elementary schools in 1891, but the cost of maintenance became a problem and the schools were made branches of the public library.

The most vital factor in the provision of books to schools was probably that of finance, and whilst J. J. Ogle regarded it as an excuse for failure to provide a library service, it certainly had validity. At Leeds the collections were well used and it was found impossible to maintain them. It was regrettable that *the* pioneer library should find it necessary to admit the impracticability of its work, but under existing conditions there appeared to be no alternative.

In spite of financial problems many schemes were successful. The Board School libraries at Plymouth were referred to in the public library annual report for 1890/91, as having given entire satisfaction, and several of the schools had applied for and received additional grants of books.

Agreements were reached as to the administration of the libraries. At Leeds and at Plymouth the books were purchased out of the public library rate whilst the school board assumed responsibility for the fittings. With very few exceptions the costs were met by public library committees at first. It became clear that the

joint schemes could only be successful if the school board was prepared to make a grant, and at Cardiff in 1898 it provided £500, a sum which was followed by recurring annual payments of £300 on a basis of 50s. for each group of 100 children in average attendance. It was customary for a joint committee to be appointed as at Cardiff and at Plymouth.

Collections in schools varied in size. The Leeds stock consisted of 7750 volumes in 1898, 10 years after its inception. The books were distributed among 39 schools, and during 1897 the issues totalled 93,257. In 1889, 14 board schools at Plymouth each contained 100 carefully selected books which were supplemented whenever possible; whilst in the same year Norwich provided libraries of a similar size in 38 elementary schools. At Cardiff in 1899 there was a total stock of 4070 volumes for the use of 5264 children in 15 elementary schools. In addition, Cardiff libraries loaned two collections to each school, one for the boys and one for the girls. Bookstocks at Cardiff increased rapidly, rising to 9550 in 1902.

The usual practice was to provide facilities for the children in standards IV to VII, and this pattern was followed at Leeds, Plymouth, Norwich, Cardiff, and Cambridge. Inquiries were made at Plymouth on behalf of the younger children, but insufficient books were available to make possible a service. The problem was not solely one of finance but of a deficiency of suitable material for younger children, a situation which was experienced at Bootle when an attempt was made to cater for pupils in standard III.

There was, however, a larger number of children who did not enjoy the advantages of public-library–school co-operation. Most of the schemes only affected the board schools, whilst the voluntary schools were often completely excluded. In 1898 there were 33 libraries in Leeds board schools and only 6 in voluntary schools. At Plymouth both board and voluntary schools housed collections from the public library, but there was no such co-operation at Cardiff at that time. Unless voluntary schools possessed their own libraries it was reasonable to assume that their pupils' primary access to books was through the public

library. The significance of an absence of library facilities in voluntary schools is realized when it is remembered that there were relatively few public libraries on a national scale which provided for children. In addition, there were in 1899 2,144,118 children in attendance at board schools and 2,500,095 at voluntary schools. It can be inferred therefore that thousands of children in both urban and rural areas had no library facilities at all.

It remains to discuss one other aspect of public-library–school co-operation. In 1896 the Committee of Council was concerned that children should regard books as being of value to them at school and should also retain their reading habits on the completion of their formal education. It was desirable that children should be aware of the facilities offered by the public library, and this was to be effected by talks and visits.

Until the Cardiff Corporation Bill received the royal assent in 1898 it was financially impossible to provide libraries in schools, but an agreement was reached with the head teachers of both board and voluntary schools in 1896 that pupils in standards IV to VII should visit the public library once in each year for a talk by the librarian.

The Committee of Council commented favourably in 1898 on the many instances in which closer connection was developing between the public libraries and the schools, and in his special report to the Education Department in that year on *The Connection between the Public Library and the Public Elementary School*, J. J. Ogle noted "abundant signs of progress".

Ballinger's work at Cardiff aroused interest in other parts of the country and similar activities were undertaken at Camberwell, Leyton, Great Yarmouth and Peterborough. School visits to public libraries were organized also at Birmingham but did not derive their inspiration from Cardiff.

It has been shown in the last chapter that the principal area where public libraries and school libraries remained separated was in London. Facilities for children in the public libraries of the capital were very few before 1890, but teachers and pupils were allowed "extra students' tickets" at the public libraries. The

librarians at West Ham and Wandsworth attempted to foster a spirit of co-operation but received no encouragement from the London School Board. However, in 1899 the Battersea public library encountered no difficulty from the school board when it offered to receive visits from children during school hours, and in due course the schools were contacted and a programme was organized.

The Golden Years of Children's Literature Part II 1890–1920

THE Golden Age in children's books continued to 1914 although the demand for fairy tales and fantasy diminished and gave place to family/adventure stories in which the morals did not obtrude. In the last two decades of the 19th century there was a sharp decline in the sales of the R.T.S. publications, which was not only contrary to the trends in secular literature but also to those in the more liberal S.P.C.K. Among the new publishers were Dent, Heinemann, Hodder & Stoughton, Methuen, and Collins, the latter of whom produced a *Catalogue of Juvenile Literature* for the first time in 1900.

Developments were arrested with the commencement of World War I in 1914 and the production of books was restricted. Paper and other raw materials became scarce, staff were enlisted or deployed to the production of munitions, and costs rose enormously. There was, however, a great demand for books, including literature for children, and in the absence of a good supply of new material, the publication of rewards became the major occupation in the publishing trade. Blackie, Collins, and Warne were representative of this enterprise, the content of which consisted mainly of adventure and school stories.

The most outstanding writer of the period was E. Nesbit, whose healthy, moral free, true to life family/adventure stories included *The Story of the Treasure Seekers* (1899) and *The Railway Children* (1906). Similarly popular were S. R. Crockett's rather sentimental *Sir Toady Lion* (1897) and *Sir Toady Crusoe* (1905) and Frances E. Crompton's *The Gentle Heritage* (1893).

Adventure stories included John Meade Falkner's *Moonfleet* (1898) which was reminiscent of *Treasure Island*, and Crockett's *The Black Douglas* (1899). As regards rewards the most prominent writers were Percy F. Westerman, who achieved a popularity comparable to that of Henty; F. S. Brereton; Herbert Strang; and Robert and Alexander MacDonald. The latter used as their backgrounds personal experiences in the Australian bush and New Guinea. World War I provided plots for adventure stories and books appeared with such titles as Percy Westerman's *Rounding Up the Raider*, Brereton's *Under Haig in Flanders*, Hayens' *Midst Shot and Shell in Flanders*, and C. T. Bridges' *With Beatty in the North Sea*. Bessie Marchant, who produced adventure stories for girls, wrote *A Dangerous Mission*.

Historical fiction was interesting in that it was more closely related to time-fantasy than to the earlier examples of J. G. Edgar, G. A. Henty and Charlotte M. Yonge. Kipling's *Puck of Pook's Hill* and *Rewards and Fairies* relied on historical personages being brought to the 20th century through the agency of Puck; whilst E. Nesbit's *The Story of the Amulet*, *The House of Arden*, and other stories depended on modern children being magically removed to other periods through the agency of the wonderful Psammead and the Mouldiwarp.

Kipling championed the school story for boys when he ridiculed Farrar's books in his *Stalky and Co.* (1899). Other writers of school stories for boys in these years were Desmond Coke, Herbert Hayens, Charles Turley, and P. G. Wodehouse, whilst for girls the leading contributors were Angela Brazil and Elsie Oxenham.

The importance of fantasy may have decreased after 1890 but a number of works were published for highly competent authors: G. E. Farrow, J. M. Barrie (Fig. 21), Laurence Housman, E. Nesbit, W. W. Tarn, Bertha Upton, and Oscar Wilde. Fairy tales and folklore too, were well represented and editors included Joseph Jacobs, Andrew Lang, Mary Macleod, W. H. D. Rouse, Ernest Rhys, and Arthur Ransome. A series which was to set standards of production was established in 1901 when the first

Fig. 21. Title page from Sir James Barrie's *Peter and Wendy*.
1911 edition.
(By courtesy of Hodder & Stoughton Ltd.)

of Dent's classics appeared in the form of an edition of Grimms' *Fairy Tales*. During the War fairy tales were particularly represented as a manifestation of escapism from an all too grim reality, and special "gift books" were utilized for the financial success of good causes such as Arthur Rackham's *Allies Fairy Book*.

Kipling demonstrated his versatility as a writer of romanticized animal stories in his Jungle Books (1894/5) and *Just So Stories* (1902); and Walter de la Mare produced *The Three Mulla-Mulgars* in 1910. It is perhaps appropriate to mention at this point, *Bevis*, the nature story by Richard Jefferies, which was first published in 1882 but was reissued in a more popular edition in 1904 by E. V. Lucas. Representative authors of fantasy animal stories were Beatrix Potter and Kenneth Grahame, whose work attained the all too rare peaks of writing for the young, and who presented to the world Peter Rabbit and Mr. Toad.

Poetry for children, which had not been widespread in the 19th century, came into its own in the work of Walter de la Mare, whose *Songs of Childhood* was published in 1902 under the pseudonym of Walter Ramal. His *A Child's Day* appeared in 1912 and *Peacock Pie* in 1913. Other poetical writing included Hilaire Belloc's *Cautionary Tales For Children* (1908) and Eleanor Farjeon's *Nursery Rhymes of London Town* (1916), which was followed in 1917 with *More Nursery Rhymes*. Outstanding anthologies were E. V. Lucas' *A Book of Verses for Children* (1897) and *Another Book of Verses for Children* (1907).

After the Chace Act of Congress in 1891 there were some noticeable changes in the importation of American books. Prices rose to a limited extent after 1891, for example Harris' *Uncle Remus* was issued by Routledge for 1*s.* that year, but between 1892 and 1897, only American editions were published in Britain at the price of 7*s.* 6*d.* per volume. However, the difference was not particularly remarkable in other cases due to the general reduction in book prices during the last decade of the old century and the first decade of the new. Outstanding books from the United States were Howard Pyle's *The Story of King Arthur and his Knights*,

Gene Stratton Porter's *A Girl of the Limberlost*, Mrs. Hodgson Burnett's *The Secret Garden*, and Padraic Colum's *Adventures of Odysseus and the Tale of Troy* which came to England in 1920.

Canada was represented by nature stories in the tradition of *Bevis*. Ernest Thompson Seton's *Two Little Savages* and *Rolf in the Woods* described life in the forest, as did his collections of *Lives of the Hunted* and *Wild Animal Ways*. Charles Roberts, another Canadian, wrote *The Kindred of the Wild* and *Red Fox*.

Helen Bannerman's *Little Black Sambo* continued the tradition established by Crane, Caldecott and Greenaway, but her work differed from that of the earlier illustrators in its small format. Bertha Upton's Golliwog books were well illustrated by Florence Upton. The most famous illustrator of picture books was Beatrix Potter, who depicted the life at Sawrey in the English Lake District in her delightful productions which were mainly published between 1902 and the World War in 1914. The important feature of these books, however, was the increased proportion of attention given to the text, whereas in the past, the books had been produced for the sake of the pictures alone. This tradition was not discontinued but was represented in the work of Leslie Brooke in his *Golden Goose Book* and *Johnny Crow's Garden*. The house of Warne was to be congratulated on the galaxy of superb craftsmen who illustrated its picture books and which included Crane, Caldecott, Greenaway, Potter and Brooke.

The introduction of three colour letterpress printing made possible a use of colour hitherto unknown in most children's books. Between 1903 and 1914, Collins produced more than 500 different colour books for young children. Well produced annuals were very fashionable due to low production costs, among which may be noted, Blackie's *Children's Annual* which first appeared at Christmas in 1904, and Collins' *Children's Annual* which was on sale from 1914, and survived the War.

Among the authors whose work began in the period prior to 1890 but who were writing after that date were L. T. Meade, Mrs. Molesworth, and Talbot Baines Reed. L. T. Meade's *Beyond the Blue Mountains* (1893) was in her words "something between an allegory and a fairy tale", whilst Reed's *The Cock House at Fellsgarth* (1891) continued the brand of school story which he had developed and would probably have maintained had it not been for his untimely death at the age of 41 in 1893. Mrs. Molesworth's *The Carved Lions* (1895) was in the opinion of Roger Lancelyn Green "probably the best book she ever wrote", a view with which the present writer is in complete agreement. Other books of note by Mrs. Molesworth were the allegorical *The Children of the Castle* (1890) and the perennially successful *The Ruby Ring* (1904).

In those days the bindings of children's books were highly decorative with gilt lettering and vignettes, the paper wrapper not as yet being in use. The illustrations were often of a high standard and among the leading artists were F. D. Bedford, C. E. and H. M. Brock, Gordon Browne, Edmund Dulac, H. J. Ford, Charles Folkard, Harry Furniss, Laurence Housman, H. R. Millar, Arthur Rackham, and the Brothers Robinson.

The supply of non-fiction books began to increase in the new century. Outstanding works in this category which could be used by children included D. C. Calthrop's *English Costume, 1066–1820* (Black, 1907); Mrs. Aeneas Gunn's *We of the Never-Never* (Hutchinson, 1908) which was concerned with Australia; H. E. Marshall's *English Literature for Boys and Girls* (Nelson, 1909); John Buchan's *Sir Walter Raleigh* (Nelson, 1911); and Quennell's *A History of Everyday Things in England* (Batsford, 1918/9). Most of these books were for the use of children aged 11 and over and in truth there were still too few books of non-fiction for younger children, for whom the most popular subject in terms of the material which was available, appeared to be nature study. Books in this category included Adelaide Austen's *Book of Favourite Animals* (Nimmo), Edith Carrington's *Peeps into Birdland* (Nelson), and J. H. Stickney's *Pets and Companions* (Ginn). There were also numerous religious books such as Mrs. Haskell's *Little Ones' Book of Bible Stories* (Blackie), V. S. Morwood's *Easy Guide to Scripture Animals* (Hogg) and R. G. Moulton's *New Testament Bible Stories* and *Old Testament Bible*

Stories (Macmillan). The R.T.S. publications, *Little Harry at the Seaside* and *Little Harry in London* by F. M. Holmes heralded a new era in "here and now" literature, but in their day did not conform to the general pattern. After the World War there was an ever-growing selection of books relating to aircraft, cars, railways and ships, a recognition of the contemporary scene which was not often evident in works of fiction.

The 1890's witnessed the triumph of the cheap book movement and, at the same time, Frederick Macmillan achieved an end to the price war in persuading publishers to divide their books into net (most children's books) and non-net (mainly school books) categories. Net books costing more than 6*s.* were not to be sold at a discount, and each publisher was to decide the retail price of his own books. In 1899, 1106 out of 1270 booksellers in the United Kingdom became signatories to the Net Book Agreement.

The S.P.C.K. met the demand for cheapness by publishing a series of penny books which included *Robinson Crusoe*, Scott's *The Talisman*, Southey's *Life of Nelson*, and various titles by Captain Marryat. In addition, a well bound series of famous books at 6*d.* was produced. These ventures were very successful as regards sales, but they involved the Society in financial losses and had to be discontinued. George Newnes' *Penny Library of Famous Books* appeared in 1896, although in some cases the novels were spread over three volumes. However, the economic problems of the War and its aftermath ended the era of cheap reprints.

New books for children showed no reduction in price and so maintained a pattern which had persisted since 1850. Joseph Jacob's *English Fairy Tales* (1890), Kipling's *The Jungle Book* (1894), Crockett's *Sir Toady Lion* (1897), E. Nesbit's *The Story of the Treasure Seekers* (1899) and *Five Children and It* (1902), and Grahame's *The Wind in the Willows* (1908), were all published at 6*s.* Slighter volumes were available at lower prices, for example Beatrix Potter's picture books sold at 1*s.* and 1*s.* 6*d.*; Brooke's *Johnny Crow's Garden* and Farjeon's *Nursery Rhymes of London Town* at 7*s.* 6*d.* Book prices were still beyond the financial resources of the working people, and with the post-1914 disappearance of very cheap reprints and the later spread of unemployment, the situation deteriorated rapidly.

A remarkable phenomenon of the later 19th century and early 20th century was the publication of adventure stories which were not written for young people but were widely adopted by teenagers. Before 1890 Arthur Conan Doyle's *A Study in Scarlet* (1887) and H. Rider Haggard's *King Solomon's Mines* (1885) achieved popular acclaim and between 1890 and 1920 a large number of authors produced work of a similar kind. Surely many of the books written in this period must have been among the most thrilling adventure stories of all time, examples of which were Buchan's *The Thirty Nine Steps*, Edgar Rice Burroughs' *Tarzan of the Apes*, Anthony Hope's *The Prisoner of Zenda*, Baroness Orczy's *The Scarlet Pimpernel*, A. E. W. Mason's *The Four Feathers*, H. S. Merriman's *Barlasch of the Guard*, Sapper's *Bulldog Drummond*, Stevenson's *St. Ives*, Edgar Wallace's *Sanders of the River*, and Wells' *War of the Worlds*. Other outstanding authors were Jeffrey Farnol, E. W. Hornung and Stanley Weyman.

It was not possible for the majority of children to purchase books even had they been inclined to do so. There was a boom in the publication of periodicals which could be bought without hardship, although the lives of the majority of these productions were short. Many of the 19th-century examples, however, continued to appear into the 20th century, such as *The Boy's Own Paper*, which had been a weekly since 1879 but became a monthly in 1913; *The Girl's Own Paper*, which became a monthly in 1908; *Chatterbox* (discontinued in 1948); and *Little Folks* (discontinued in 1931).

Comic strips were inaugurated by Harmsworth's *Comic Cuts* (1890–1953), which was at first intended for semi-literate adults, but was later adapted for children. In his campaign against the "penny dreadful", Harmsworth, in 1914, launched *The Rainbow* (discontinued in 1956), in the strips of which right always triumphed, and a level of satire was discovered which appealed to children, more successfully than any previous literature. The vocabulary of the Harmsworth *Rainbow* was regarded as adequate to the needs of children in the age group of 5 to 7 for which it catered. Harmsworth's Amalgamated Press, which grew out of Answers Publications Ltd. in 1902, had no serious competitors for many years.

These papers were subjected to severe criticism by many, but the Newbolt Committee on *The Teaching of English in England* (1921) considered that

> ... the fear that the children of today are being demoralized or exposed to evil suggestion by the penny stories and penny magazines which they devour in such large quantities is, in our belief, a mistaken one.

It was admitted, however, that the Committee had "discovered below these, a stratum of very different matter, where stories of crude sensationalism are told in a jargon of degrading slang". In contrast to the opinions of earlier generations, it was not thought that the "dreadfuls" could effect a great deal of harm as their contents did "not appear to be popular among children".

Two outstanding periodical publications which were singled out for particular praise by the Newbolt Committee were *My Magazine* and *The Children's Newspaper*, both of which were edited by Arthur Mee. The former began as *The Children's Encyclopaedia* in 1908, which was issued in 50 fortnightly parts, and was followed in 1910 with *The New Children's Encyclopaedia* (monthly). The title was changed in 1911 to *The Children's Magazine*, in 1914 to *My Children's Magazine*, and in 1915 to *My Magazine*, which title it bore until it was discontinued in 1933. *The Children's Newspaper*, on the other hand, commenced publication in 1919 and continued until 1965, although Arthur Mee's editorship ceased in 1943.

CHAPTER 14

Educational Progress and Practice 1902–1918

AFTER 1902 the centre of interest was transferred from elementary education to instruction in secondary schools. The Board of Education reversed the policy of the late Committee of Council in its intention to guide development rather than to dictate its views. Previously requirements had been detailed in the Instructions to Inspectors, but in 1905 the new attitude was manifested in the Board's *Suggestions for the Consideration of Teachers . . . in Public Elementary Schools,* although a series of regulations were also issued for both elementary and secondary schools. The Local Education Authorities (L.E.A.s) were more likely to respond to this more favourable relationship than would have been possible with the multiplicity of school boards after 1870. The years after 1902 were important to education in Wales, as in 1907 the Board created a separate Welsh Department and a new emphasis was given to instruction in Welsh subjects.

The concept of elementary education as a charity was held no longer in responsible circles, as was evidenced in the Code of 1904 which stated that:

> . . . the purpose of the public elementary school is to form and strengthen the character and to develop the intelligence of the children entrusted to it, and to make the best use of the school years available, in assisting both girls and boys, according to their different needs, to fit themselves practically as well as intellectually, for the work of life . . .

This theme was developed in a parliamentary speech by H. A. L. Fisher in 1917 when he claimed:

> There is a growing sense, not only in England but through Europe . . . that the industrial workers of the country are entitled to be considered

primarily as citizens and as fit subjects for any form of education from which they are capable of profiteering [*sic*].

He added:

> They do not want education only in order that they may become better technical workmen, and earn higher wages. They do not want it in order that they may rise out of their own class, always a vulgar ambition, they want it because they know that in the treasures of the mind they can find an aid to good citizenship, a source of pure enjoyment and a refuge from the necessary hardships of life spent in the midst of clanging machinery in our hideous cities of toil.

In actual fact large numbers of working people and their children have used education as a means to the fulfilment of their "vulgar ambition", and Fisher probably had his own reasons for fearing this social tendency, but there can be no doubt that a distinct change of attitude had taken place on the part of the leaders of the community to the needs of the masses.

Measures were taken to regulate the attendance at school of children between 1902 and 1920. The Employment of Children Act of 1903 empowered L.E.A.s to specify the minimum age at which children could be employed out of school hours, and the Prevention of Cruelty to Children Act of 1904 further restricted their employment. The Fisher Education Act of 1918 enabled L.E.A.s to raise the school leaving age to 15 and abolished all exemptions from attendance for children under 14. Half-time instruction was not completely superseded, however, until July 1922.

An interest in the education of children from their earliest years was witnessed in the institution of the nursery school in 1911 at Deptford by Rachel and Margaret McMillan, which was probably the best known example of its kind. At first the endeavour was voluntary, but in the Fisher Act it became permissible for L.E.A.s to establish nursery schools. Grants for this purpose became available in 1919 but progress was and has remained slow.

As children passed through the elementary school the Code of 1904 stipulated that those who showed exceptional ability should be groomed for transfer to secondary schools "and be able to derive the maximum benefit from the education there offered them". The Regulations for Secondary Schools of 1904 made certain that the new county secondary institutions should be moulded in the pattern of the public and grammar schools and that specialization should be preceded by general education. The hours to be devoted to each subject were detailed to ensure the maintenance of a balance, but this was rescinded in 1907, in which year Supplementary Regulations decreed that all secondary schools in receipt of grants from the Board must provide free places for 25 % of their annual intake. This then was the beginning of the scholarship system which would provide access from elementary school to university.

In 1894 only 4 or 5 pupils per 1000 in the elementary schools passed to the secondary schools, but by 1911 the proportion of the population receiving full-time education between the ages of 14 and 18 had doubled. In 1906 there were 23,000 awards covering all or part of fees, but many authorities were not providing any scholarships. In 1913 the awards had increased to 60,000.

In spite of this encouraging development in secondary education the majority of children were not receiving adequate instruction and there was a need for an extended system of further education for those who left school at 14. Further education was principally organized by mechanics' institutes, polytechnics, and trades unions' and workers' educational organizations in the earlier years of the 20th century. Progressive firms such as Rowntree (1905), Cadbury (1906) and Reckitt and Colman, sponsored it unofficially. For example, Cadbury's required all their young workers to attend evening classes from 1906 but in 1913 day release was introduced, it being considered unfair to expect staff to study at the end of a day's work. Government interest was shown in 1909 when the Board of Education's Consultative Committee pronounced in favour of compulsory part-time day education to the age of 17, but by 1911/12 there were approximately 2,700,000 juveniles aged 14 to 18 of whom 81 % were enrolled in neither day nor evening schools. The 1918 Act stipulated that continuation schools should be a compulsory feature of educational provision, but this was not enforced, with the exception of work undertaken at Rugby, due to the post-war depression.

Legislation in 1914 compelled L.E.A.s to make suitable provision for mentally defective and epileptic children. The work of Maria Montessori with mentally defective children became known in England and as regards her emphasis on the training of the senses, her ideas were applied to normal children. Her book *The Montessori Method* was translated into English in 1912.

There was a gradual development in instructional methods which was closely related to the ideas of the educational psychologists, of whom William James and William McDougall were leading figures. *Social Psychology* by McDougall was published in 1908. The psychologists pointed out that children should not be expected to attain a prescribed level of ability as had been believed formerly, but that teaching must be geared to the abilities, experience and interests of each child at each stage of his growth. The group and individual methods of Dalton and Dewey were therefore introduced and where they were adopted completely revolutionized the old routines of class teaching. Children were to be trained "in habits of observation and clear reasoning, so that they might gain an acquaintance with some of the facts and laws of nature" (1904 Code), and were to learn by discovery. In such an organization the teacher would observe and direct but never dictate the activities of the children.

Intelligence tests were developed to ascertain the level of individual ability. In 1914, Ballard published the first standardized scale in reading, and in 1917, Cyril Burt reported the results of a survey undertaken in London. The growth of literacy, therefore, was to be based on systematic investigations, and children were to be considered as individual contributors to the national level of literacy rather than a mass to be humanized as little as possible.

There were two principal reasons why the education of the people had to be accelerated after the cessation of hostilities in 1918. Firstly, Britain was to be faced with increased international competition in the economic sector; and secondly, the extension of the franchise to all men over 21 and all women over 30 in the

Representation of the People Act of 1918 was destined to make "a greater demand than ever before upon the civic spirit of the ordinary man and woman" (Fisher).

The new attitude in education necessarily involved a more meaningful use of books. An interest was to be aroused in children in elementary schools "in the ideals and achievements of mankind", and they were to be made aware of the literary and historical traditions of their country. This would be partially effected if a taste for good reading was developed, which together with a critical approach to study would enable them to increase their knowledge in later years (Elementary Code, 1904).

Facilities were to be made available for children to read at their desks books which interested them, at such times as they were not undergoing formal instruction. At a more advanced level, that is at the secondary or university stage, the accepted method of study was to combine the study of a lesson in class with wider general reading at home, and there was no valid reason why this idea should not be extended to the elementary school. The primary difference, however, was that the discipline of general reading would be undertaken at school rather than at home (Suggestions, 1905).

Admittedly, for the majority of children, the English course would secure solely the ability to speak, read, and write with moderate fluency, intelligence and accuracy. At this time the favoured method of instruction in reading was through phonics, and the principal aim was to enable pupils "to master printed or written matter for their own information". Silent reading was encouraged, especially in the higher standards, and comprehension was ensured by a paraphrased feedback on the part of the pupils. It was also useful for children to be trained in oral reading so that the teacher and other pupils could understand what was being read without using copies of the book themselves. The criticism which had been levelled during the 19th century that children did not read with expression, had given rise in many schools to the use of declamation and gesture, a practice which was frequently taken to extremes of absurdity. Whilst it seemed difficult to obtain a reasonable balance, dramatization was certainly not required in the intelligent reading of literature.

An emphasis on the provision of books was made increasingly in the years prior to 1914. It was stipulated in Article 20 of the Code for 1906 that "the school must be adequately and suitably equipped with the apparatus requisite for its curriculum, including desks, furniture, books and maps". In the Code for 1907, however, the same Article was elaborated to read that:

> Provision should be made for securing an adequate supply of suitable books for the course of general reading in the higher classes of the school, and for bringing to the scholars such agencies as may assist them in the continuation of their studies in after life. Dictionaries and atlases should be provided for older scholars.

Article 20 continued to be phrased in this form with only small modifications until 1925.

There was evidence in the movement towards technological education after 1880 of a body of opinion which was critical of the use of books. The "bookish" training received by teachers, however, often resulted in science teaching consisting principally of textbook memorizing with little or no practical work, and geography required little more than the learning of lists of names. In the early years of the new century attempts had been made to provide adequately equipped science laboratories, and geography became more closely related to "the world of nature as distinct from the world of books" (Suggestions, 1905). The need was stated in the Code of 1904, for children to be trained to observe and to draw conclusions relating to "the facts and laws of nature". Practical work was designed to develop manual and visual dexterity. Such an education, it was argued, would not be criticized on the grounds that an undue emphasis was attached to the use of books. Experience had shown that if badly taught, natural history would soon degenerate into reading instead of observation and activity. If books were to be used at all therefore, they must be used sparingly and should contain records of first hand observations by scientists rather than "mere accounts put together y a compiler" (Suggestions, 1905).

The individual use of books was subjected to particular criticism in the case of children under 7. This was not unreasonable, as most of them would not have mastered the mechanics of reading, even had suitably adapted literature been available. They were encouraged to ask questions and were told the myths of Greece and Rome and other epics of history and legend, which would prepare them for the more recent exploits of Columbus and Nansen. It was helpful for children to listen to accounts of "Red Indians and their wigwams, Eskimos and their snow huts". Similarly, in history, the instruction was to be purely oral and attention given to storytelling.

The result of the official attitude was a movement away from the use of books, and attempts were subsequently made to redress the balance. The absence of books in science teaching was deplored in the Board's pamphlet *Natural Science in Education* (1918):

> There is a tendency at present in some cases to discourage boys from reading anything about their science work except the notes which they take in class and in the laboratory. We consider that this policy is most pernicious. If a boy is interested in his subject he will naturally wish to read about it and should be encouraged to do so. A part of the time given to preparation, which is now often devoted to the mere transcription of laboratory notes, might be spent in this way, and the boys should have access to good scientific books suitable to the stage of knowledge reached. The practice of discouraging private reading is responsible for the tendency, which has become more noticeable in recent years, for students of science at the universities to rely entirely on the instruction they get in lectures. Some of them seem to have lost any desire to read for themselves and for want of practice lack the ability to use books to any advantage. Boys who have acquired the habit of reading books of science when at school are more likely to keep alive in after-life their knowledge and interest in the subject.

The absence of any reference to girls is a commentary on the official attitude to their education in 1918. It is to be recognized without a doubt, however, that the absence of books was viewed with grave concern by those who had previously instigated their relegation to a subsidiary position in educational method.

Of equal importance with the methods of using books was their selection. The minimum of two or three reading books as prescribed in earlier Codes was no longer adequate, and whilst financial considerations could obstruct a more liberal provision, it was possible to operate a system of interchanges of books between different classes. Reading books were to contain stories and passages of literary value only, and at least one should be a continuous text to be examined for both its subject matter and its form.

Educational publishers continued to expand their business to meet new demands in elementary and secondary education. Blackie issued books on a variety of subjects including *The Little French Classics* (from 1901), W. H. D. Rouse's *English Texts* (from 1904), *The Plain-Text Shakespeare* (1906), *Model Poetry Books* (1907), *Lands and their Stories* (1909), *Regional Geographies* (1911), *Britain and her Neighbours* (1913). A particularly famous text of these years was Warner and Marten's *The Groundwork of British History* (1911).

The contemporary restriction of books which was applied to younger children was not considered relevant to the needs of older pupils. In geography, children of 10+ were encouraged to read for themselves books of travel which related to their lessons, whilst in history a well chosen book was to be provided to supplement oral lessons when children were 9 years old. It was acknowledged that history was a subject which offered opportunities for the training of children in silent reading and well selected books were of primary importance. "Technical phraseology" and "childish simplicity" were to be avoided in books.

The school could not develop expertise and taste in reading without assistance. Where parents co-operated by encouraging their children to read at home, this was an invaluable help to those who had insufficient practice in overcrowded classes. The National Home Reading Union, to which reference has already been made, was instrumental in continuing the work of the schools, and it was possible for middle-class children to form reading circles. In the case of poorer children, teachers frequently established circles at school which were held during the evening. Public libraries often helped in this connection by supplying books recommended by the Union, by publicizing its aims, and by offering help and advice in the formation of circles. There was no necessity for children to confine their reading to literary subjects, but with increased maturity they could study geography, history, politics, and other topics.

In 1909 the West Riding Education Committee introduced a scheme for the encouragement of reading among elementary school children. Voluntary reading groups were formed in which either each child purchased a book which was circulated among the other members and kept by the last reader or the original owner; or a number of copies of one book were acquired which formed the basis for discussion. The Education Committee compiled lists of suitable books with the assistance of teachers and made books available at discounts of 33 % in some cases and 50 % in instances where a number of copies of one book were required. The scheme was introduced into 532 schools, 64 of which were added in 1912/13. Books were mainly English classics and standard authors, but some geography, history, nature study and even fairy tales were included.

Schools were often irresponsible in the methods they used to further reading and the use of books. It was the custom in schools provided by the London County Council and other local education authorities to award book prizes for various merits, but the books which were selected were not necessarily of a high standard or of lasting value. A waste of public money was surely involved where books were only likely to have an immediate rather than a long-term appeal to their recipients. Many schools, however, awarded works of reference or the writings of standard authors in good quality editions which would be useful in adult life and be sources of increasing pleasure or profit to their owners.

CHAPTER 15

Libraries for Children
1902–1919

A GREAT deal of information relating to libraries in schools during the 19th century was to be derived from the Minutes and Reports of the Committee of Council on Education, but after 1899 the annual reports of the Board of Education were far less exhaustive, and yielded little more than statistical tables. In 1902 there were 8504 libraries in 20,153 elementary schools, and in 1905 there were not more than 9000. Therefore in the early years of the century approximately 45% of the elementary schools contained libraries.

Birmingham was one of the new L.E.A.s which made grants for the provision of libraries in schools. Some of the county education committees were also active in this respect. A scheme was commenced in Cumberland in 1909 by which boxes of books were circulated around schools and were changed on three or four occasions in a year. In 1912/13 a grant of £20 was made by the Buckinghamshire Education Committee for the supply of books to 30 schools in the county area, and at Norfolk in 1913 all 491 schools in the county (with the exception of those served by good public libraries) were in receipt of boxes of books.

The Board of Education's *Suggestions for Teachers* (1905) advocated the use of school libraries by older pupils in their study of geography and history. In a joint report of librarians and educational authorities to the London County Council in 1907 it was acknowledged that the problem lay not so much in the provision of books but in the inculcation of a habit of reading in children from the age of 7, and they could only envisage a task of such magnitude being accomplished if it were entrusted to teachers. Many people believed that reading facilities for children of school age should be provided only in school libraries.

Unfortunately many school libraries were not fulfilling their functions satisfactorily, and books for use in schools on L.E.A. requisition lists were often quite unsuitable for children. Particularly noticeable was the absence of books adapted for younger children aged between 7 and 12, who having mastered the mechanics of reading were not given adequate opportunity to develop their interests. The joint committee of librarians and teachers in London undertook a revision of the L.C.C. list and ensured that most of the recommended books were inspected individually.

During the years from 1850 to 1909, 522 towns adopted the Public Libraries Act, a total which was completely inadequate for the requirements of the nation, and which could well have been doubled. For large numbers of children the public library was the only place where they could read due to poor domestic environments and the absence of libraries in schools. In 1903, John Ballinger drew attention to the needs of thousands of children who were "not only incurring danger to health" but were also "making companionships and forming habits injurious to them". Their homes were small and badly lighted, they had no books and very often their families were "out of sympathy with their desire to read".

The joint committee in its report to the L.C.C. in 1907 listed what it considered to be the functions of public libraries in the provision of

1. a place for reading by children in the evenings, on Saturdays, and during school holidays;
2. books for home reading;
3. skilled advice for children regarding their choice of books;
4. books for reference in connection with school work;
5. specially adapted sets of books for loans to schools.

It was wrong to assume that all children would wish to read for pleasure and it was necessary to attract those who would read for information relating to practical interests. The function of children's libraries was to be interpreted too in the light of the new ideas of the educational psychologists, which entailed the provision of facilities for self-development.

There was some opposition to the special provision of library services for children as there had been since their inception. Critics contended that one library and one reading room should serve *all*, but as this would inconvenience adult users, children under 16 must be excluded. The librarian of Peterborough in 1907 complained that children did not read when they visited a library but turned the pages "in feverish haste" and maintained "a ceaseless fire of chatter". Perhaps more serious than opposition was the more widespread spirit of indifference. Whilst some libraries were reasonably adequate in their provision others were neglected and as a contribution to the national economy in 1917 the children's rooms at Manchester were closed. In these years the advent of the cinema was regarded as a threat to the success of children's libraries.

Supporters of library work with children drew their inspiration from the United States where in many places excellent children's rooms were in existence. Ballinger commented that "until our financial resources are improved, we can only hope to follow humbly in the footsteps of such magnificent institutions as the Carnegie libraries of Pittsburgh". In the United States special librarians underwent training for the work, and as early as 1898 a course on library work with young people was available at the Pratt Institute. A Children's Library Association was founded in 1905 and there was an abundance of enthusiasm. The facilities were attractive and bookshelves were placed around the walls, whilst in the centres of the rooms were chairs and tables which had been designed on a smaller scale than usual for the convenience of the children. "But", said Ballinger (who was now librarian of the National Library of Wales), "children's rooms cannot be established in this country because we cannot afford them out of the rates". However, the provision in the United States was uneven, and whilst Ballinger could point to models for possible emulation, it is true that vast tracts of that large country were devoid of library services until the late 1950's.

In view of the financial disadvantages in Britain it was necessary to establish priorities of provision and of these the first was books which could either be read in the library or at home, and also periodicals. Books which included illustrations were popular with children. At Peterborough, where a room for children was opened in 1905, a supply of new periodicals was maintained which included among others, *Chatterbox*, *The Child's Companion*, *Little Folks* and *Sunday Sunshine*. In addition some were transferred from the general reading room, such as *The Daily Graphic*, *Illustrated London News*, *The Boy's Own Paper*, *The Girl's Own Paper*, *Cassell's Magazine*, *Good Words*, *The Strand Magazine*, *The Windsor Magazine*, and *The Wide World*. Here then was an opportunity for children not only to become acquainted with good quality magazines, but also to read many of the serials by outstanding writers for the young which so often appeared in this form.

There were very few aids to book selection. Between 1914 and 1916 an attempt was made to include a selection of outstanding children's books in *The Library Association Record*. In 1916 the task became the responsibility of the editor of *The Athenaeum*, but only 110 titles were listed in 17 months, many of which were unsuitable for children. Recommendations were made for the establishment of a special committee of the Library Association to evaluate children's books, the results of which could be listed either in the *Record* or in a separate pamphlet. In 1918 it was possible to obtain guidance of varying degrees of value in *The Athenaeum*, *The Publishers' Circular*, and *The English Catalogue of Books*. Some public libraries had produced lists, a useful example being the Finsbury Public Library *Handbook to Juvenile Literature* (1906). In addition, local education authority requisition lists were available as were publishers' catalogues.

Second in importance to a well-selected stock was the presence of a suitably qualified staff. The problem of children's behaviour at Peterborough would not have existed had competent staff been available. Ballinger advocated "a sympathetic, well-educated woman, with organizing ability and a good temper". Suitable staff would require reasonable working conditions and a salary commensurate with their responsibilities if they were to be attracted to children's work. Lady Superintendents were appointed at Cardiff in 1907, and as late as 1917 one enthusiast complained that he knew of no other town where a similar action had been taken. In actual fact there had been a children's librarian at Nottingham for approximately 20 years. Appointments were made at Coventry and Leeds in 1919.

The emphasis on psychology and the importance of the individual in educational circles were considered by some to be relevant to the qualifications of children's librarians. It was surely as necessary for a librarian working with children to be as well informed in child psychology as a school teacher. The reading of children must be related to their development, and only a specialist could provide relevant guidance. Many educationists were critical of the use of books and called for greater stress on observation and practical activities. Ballinger agreed at the annual meeting of the Library Association in 1917 that "education by books alone will not produce the well-educated man or woman", but he commented that "neglect of the influence of books inevitably means the loss of many things which are essential". In this he was striking a reasonable balance, a feat of which many educationists at that time seemed incapable.

In an attempt to overcome financial obstacles, Ballinger instituted reading halls which he reserved for children under 16 years of age. The halls were open from 4.30 to 8.30 p.m. on weekdays, and from 11 a.m. to 8.30 p.m. on Saturdays and other school holidays. At Bristol, tables were provided for children in the public libraries but not separate rooms. The room at Peterborough was made possible with a Carnegie grant of £6000, which was used to defray the costs of a new building in 1905. In a survey of library provision for children in the north-west in 1911, it was discovered that of 23 libraries which were investigated, 20 had separate collections or departments in the central or branch libraries.

The dream of an ideal situation was expressed by the Joint committee in its report to the L.C.C.:

> That this conference is of the opinion that special children's rooms containing books for lending and a selection of reference books should be provided in connection with all public libraries.

In 1917, L. S. Jast, a prominent public librarian, pictured the reality as "a series of forms or desks all facing one way . . . and a desk at the top for the librarian". He concurred with the view first voiced by Ballinger approximately 15 years earlier, in advocating a system of open access, with shelves around the walls and comfortable tables and chairs, flowers and pictures. Ballinger declared that the rooms must be spacious, well lighted, warmed and ventilated, with a generous allocation of floor space of 100–160 yards. Near the entrance he would provide washing facilities because, whilst it was important for children to have clean hands, it was more important that they should not be banned from the library until they had complied with this rule. The aim was to teach children to regard the room as their own so that in time they would learn to use it freely and wisely.

Experiments were made by librarians to encourage children to read. Study circles were formed, story hours were instituted, and brief lists of books of special interest to children were compiled, in the first decade of the 20th century. At Southport in 1905 a bookmark was distributed to children on which were listed rules relating to the care of books. Special lectures were commenced at Liverpool in 1906, which were illustrated with lantern slides. Lectures were also held at Croydon and Hampstead, not only for younger children, but also for those who had recently left school. On these occasions, large audiences of children gathered at the libraries.

The principal obstacle to an effective library service was still one of finance. At Birmingham in 1919 the 1*d.* rate produced over £16,000, and the addition of another penny for library purposes would ensure the provision of all that was envisaged at that time. In 1919 a Public Libraries Act was passed as a result of which the rate limitation was removed completely, and for the first time the provision of children's libraries on a large scale became a distinct possibility.

Another feature of the Act was the power given to county councils to become library authorities for their areas. The powers were to be delegated to the education committee, a step which placed both educational and library organizations under one government. This law applied also to county boroughs which were constituted after 1919. There was, therefore, the opportunity for provision in rural areas on an unprecedented scale. It has been shown that schemes of book provision had been in operation through the agency of L.E.A.s for many years in Buckinghamshire, Cumberland, Norfolk, and the West Riding.

The Public Libraries Act of 1892 had applied to rural parishes but the rate limitation rendered its terms inoperable. In a report to the Carnegie United Kingdom Trust in 1915, Professor W. G. S. Adams of Oxford suggested the establishment of experimental libraries in counties. As a result of this an approach was made to Staffordshire which accepted the proposal whilst a similar suggestion to Oxfordshire was rejected. As the Staffordshire scheme met with success grants were requested of the Trust and received by Buckinghamshire, Gloucestershire, Somerset, Warwickshire and Wiltshire. Grants were also made by the Trust to the boroughs of Kendal and Worksop for the provision of services in surrounding rural areas.

The Adams Report revealed that in 1914, 38 % of the population of England did not have public library facilities. In Wales the figure was 54 %. Between 1915 and 1919 the Carnegie Trustees spent £132,000 on the experimental schemes. Tribute must be paid to the work of the C.U.K.T. before and after 1919 in the development of county libraries. At the same time, the Library Association and the library profession as a whole must be condemned for their complete indifference to contemporary needs and developments.

In an address to the Library Association conference in 1917, Lord Bryce stated that:

> The connection between schools and libraries must be, and ought to be very close indeed. One of the principal proofs that schools have succeeded in their work, is that people have taken to reading.

It was regarded as an advantage after 1902 to have the library and the school controlled in so many instances by the same local authorities, and this attitude was of course reinforced as regards county areas in 1919. The Adult Education Committee's Third Interim Report on *Libraries and Museums* in the latter year commented that:

> A greater call than in the past will undoubtedly be made upon our educational resources and the necessity will arise for that close co-operation between educational institutions and libraries, which is admittedly desirable in the case of school pupils if the school and the library are to fulfil their functions.

However, just as libraries for children were opposed, so public-library–school co-operation was criticized unfavourably. At a conference of library and educational authorities in Birmingham in 1906, the librarian of Aston Manor expressed the opinion that school libraries resulted in the withdrawal of children from public libraries, a factor which would be detrimental to the continuation of their reading habits as adults. In contrast, the children's libraries at Walthamstow were in 1914 transferred to the L.E.A.

Where children's work was regarded as a co-operative venture it was usual for contacts to be made between librarians and teachers. At Cardiff, the Lady Superintendent was expected to devote four mornings in each week to visiting schools for the purpose of arranging co-operative activities.

Co-operation took three principal forms: the encouragement of children in schools to use the public library, visits of classes of children to the public library, and the provision of collections of books to schools.

At Lincoln in 1903 the library committee gave head teachers in the elementary schools the option of recommending 5% of their pupils aged 10 and over for library membership. Within a month more than 100 children were enrolled in this way. The restriction as regards numbers was made due to a lack of accommodation in the library.

The Bolton Education Committee issued a four-page circular entitled *Notice to Parents Regarding Scholars' Libraries*, which was distributed in the day schools of the town. This document contained information and advice on the benefits of reading, the role of parents in encouraging home reading, and the procedure to be followed in joining the public library. At Halifax at least one visit was made to the public library under the supervision of a teacher by children who were about to leave school.

The principle of class visits to public libraries was effected in a number of instances. At Cardiff the reading halls were used for special demonstrations to visiting classes in school hours, and visits of this kind were organized at Croydon, Peterborough, Poplar, Tottenham and Wolverhampton between 1902 and 1919. At Poplar from 1915 private study classes were held in the library for periods of one hour on Monday and Wednesday mornings.

After 1902 an increasing number of towns in the country undertook co-operative schemes of book provision to schools on the pattern established by Cardiff and other pioneers, which were operated by education committees in conjunction with library committees. Work of this kind took place at Bournemouth, Bradford, Croydon, Greenwich, Halifax, Middlesbrough, Oxford, Sheffield, Southport, Tottenham and Worcester. The provision of books to schools in counties has already been noted, particularly in Westmorland where the Kendal public library was the agency involved in the provision of books with money granted by the county education committee. In most instances the education committee provided the financial support whilst the public library undertook the administrative work of the supervision and physical maintenance of the collections, and in addition joint committees were frequently appointed. However, cases may be cited where the management of the school library was the responsibility of the head teacher. Sometimes collections were circulated around a number of schools as at Croydon and Cardiff, whilst at Halifax the collections were permanent. Catalogues were often issued for the guidance of teachers.

Perhaps the most outstanding success was in London where co-operation had not previously involved the provision of books, particularly in the days of the School Board prior to 1902. A proposal by the public librarian to supply books to schools in Greenwich was submitted to the L.C.C. and adopted in 1908. A list of over 200 books was compiled and a copy was sent to each teacher who wished to participate in the scheme. In 1913 school libraries were provided in each of 48 boys' and girls' schools in Tottenham. The pattern which was to emerge was that of schools with permanent collections, supplemented for various reasons by books from public libraries.

The provision of books was not limited to children's literature. The Board of Education in its *Suggestions for Teachers* (1905) recommended that standard works such as the historical master-pieces of J. A. Froude and Lord Macaulay could be obtained from the public library. It was considered important for older children to be acquainted with material of this kind and for them not to be restricted to the use of school textbooks.

In 1911 a survey of library work with schools in the north-west revealed that in the 23 libraries questioned:

    9 supplied books to schools;
    5 provided accommodation where children could undertake homework;
   20 issued special tickets for teachers and students;
    3 loaned stereoscopic views and museum objects;
    5 received visits for talks from groups of school children;
    8 set up exhibitions of books and other materials;
  18 produced topical or subject lists of books.

Only 5 of these libraries received financial help which ranged from £10 per annum at Bootle, to £60 at Wallasey. Other libraries in this category were Ashton in Makerfield (£20–£40), Southport (£50) and Warrington (a special grant from the local authority).

Seventeen of the twenty-three were represented on the local education committee. The need was for more substantial grants, as in practice it will be seen that the removal of the rate limitation in the 1919 Public Libraries Act could not be immediately effective.

CHAPTER 16

Years of Decision in Education 1918–1945

WORLD WAR I ended with mourning, on the one hand, for the unprecedented slaughter which had taken place, but with hope, on the other, for the brave new world which was to be created. During 1919/20 there was practically no unemployment in spite of the release of returning servicemen. Prices and wages rose until they were three times their pre-war level. Then in 1921/22 prices collapsed, wages fell and unemployment rose to more than 2 million. The depression heralded an economy drive and among other recommendations made in 1921 by Sir Eric Geddes' Committee on *National Expenditure* was one which reduced educational grants by 33%. Thus within 4 years of the armistice, the prospects of educational development as envisaged in the Fisher Act were nullified.

However, the years between the two World Wars were not stagnant and evidence of a vast upsurge of ideas was witnessed in a number of reports issued by the Consultative Committees of the Board of Education. The most prominent of these documents were produced by a succession of committees under the chairmanship of Sir Henry Hadow on *The Education of the Adolescent* (1926), *Books in Public Elementary Schools* (1928), *The Primary School* (1931), and *Infant and Nursery Schools* (1933). In addition may be cited Sir Henry Newbolt's committee on *The Teaching of English in England* (1921) and Sir Patrick Spens' *Secondary Education* (1938).

The reports were filled with ideas, for example the report on *The Education of the Adolescent* advocated a complete break at

11 + between primary and secondary education and the raising of the school leaving age to 15; the report on *The Primary School* focused attention on the child rather than on instruction and contained suggestions which would transform the old elementary school into a modern primary school; whilst that on *Secondary Education* recommended the development of secondary technical schools, envisaged a tripartite system at the secondary stage, and called for the raising of the school leaving age to 16.

Further unsuccessful attempts were made to pass and activate legislation. An effort to raise the school leaving age to 15 was made in 1929 but by this time the economic crisis, which had been less marked throughout the middle years of the decade, had grown to such proportions that the plan was doomed from its inception. Unemployment rose and remained close to 3 million until 1933 but by 1937 it had fallen to approximately 1,300,000. Corresponding to the measure of improvement, an Education Act was passed in 1936 which affected to raise the school leaving age to 15 from 1939. This clause was, however, largely neutralized by an exemption for children over 14 years who were entering "beneficial employment", and rendered inoperative by the outbreak of war.

World War II was disastrous to the national system of education. Children were evacuated to areas where it was hoped they would be safe from attack from an airborne enemy. The immediate problem was to provide sufficient school places for children in the centres to which they were evacuated. Shift systems were instituted and the result was a reduction in the hours of instruction received by each child. In other cases the evacuees were placed in totally unsuitable halls or absorbed into hitherto overcrowded classes. Not all the children were evacuated and in January 1940 the percentage which remained in Liverpool was 62% whilst the national average was 80%. Many of the schools had been requisitioned by the Government and either the children of an area were crowded into one school or a scheme of home instruction was undertaken.

Meanwhile plans were discussed for the future. In 1941 a

Memorandum was prepared which was known as *The Green Book*, and in 1943 proposals were crystallized in the officially accepted White Paper on *Educational Reconstruction*. The institution of a tripartite system of secondary education (grammar, modern, technical) was recommended in the report of the Norwood Committee on *Curriculum and Examinations in Secondary Schools*, which was also published in 1943, and the plea was made that:

> In the youth of the nation we have our greatest national asset. Even on the basis of mere expediency, we cannot afford not to develop this asset to the greatest advantage.

It was in this belief that the Butler Education Act of 1944 was passed, and the system of national education co-ordinated. A Minister of Education was appointed, advisory councils were set up, and counties and county boroughs were to be L.E.A.s for all forms of public education. Three stages of instruction were recognized: primary, secondary, and further, and separate schools were to be provided for each. Whilst the general pattern in the post-war years was to sponsor the tripartite system in secondary schools, the Act was non-committal in this respect, simply stating that education was to be geared to "age, ability and aptitude". The compulsory school age was defined as "any age between 5 and 15" (a development timed for 1945 but delayed until 1947) and it was agreed that the age should be raised to 16 at an unspecified date in the future. The abolition of all fees in L.E.A. schools was also effected.

In the years between the wars the interest in the education of the individual was developed. The idea was demonstrated ably by Sir Percy Nunn in his *Education: its data and first principles* (1920), in which he claimed that "Individuality is the ideal of life". This was recognized also in the attainment tests of Ballard, Binet, Burt, Cattell, Schonell, Simon, and others. It was obvious of course that important as the individual was, he must be considered in relation to his environment. This point was made by John Dewey in *The School and Society* (1900), and 40 years later by Sir Fred Clarke in *Education and Social Change*. The Hadow report on *The Primary School* described the purpose of the curriculum as not only

> ... lessons to be mastered, but as providing fields of new and interesting experience to be explored; it appeals less to passive obedience and more to the sympathy, social spirit and imagination of the children, relies less on mass instruction and more on the encouragement of the individual, and group work.

The curriculum was to be "thought of in terms of activity and experience rather than of knowledge to be acquired and facts to be stored".

This view of education was reaffirmed by the Spens Committee. Learning in the narrower sense was more important in the secondary than in the primary school, but it was essential that studies for older children should be more closely related to daily life. A manifestation of this attitude was demonstrated in the emphasis given to general science at that time. At the outbreak of war in 1939, many schools had become "child centred" and thinking was related to ability, experience and personal interests in the attention given to group and individual methods.

The Codes of 1904 to 1926 had been concerned with fitting children according to their different needs "for the work of life". By the late 1930's the pattern of life had changed radically, and in the *Suggestions for the Consideration of Teachers* (1937) it was stated that "education must take account of leisure no less than work". The world was becoming more complex than ever before, social contacts were increasing in frequency and variety, the traditional, social and national barriers were less distinct, mobility of labour was more common. It was necessary, therefore, for people to be more adaptable and in this cause, the aim of education must be to develop to the full the potential of every child.

Education could not begin too soon. The origins of nursery schools have been traced. In 1923 Margaret McMillan founded the Nursery School Association, and in 1933 the Hadow Committee reported on *Infant and Nursery Schools*. Attention was given to the education of children under 5 in 1944, but unfortunately development in this sphere was not maintained in succeeding years.

The Hadow Committee on *The Education of the Adolescent* in 1926, recommended that all children who did not proceed to secondary schools (grammar) should nevertheless be given some form of secondary education "in the truer and broader sense of the word". Spens complained that there was in fact no clear line of demarcation between pupils at grammar and senior schools and the existing line was "always artificial and often mistaken". Through the years the secondary school population increased until in 1938 there were approximately six times as many pupils aged 14 and over than there had been in 1894, and three times as many as in 1911.

Provision for special education was also expanded. It became common after World War I for mentally defective children to be distinguished from the educationally backward. A *Mental Deficiency Committee* report in 1929 advocated, however, that both groups should be regarded as one unit and where possible educated in ordinary schools. This view was not shared by teachers who were aware of the difficulties involved in such a situation. After 1944 L.E.A.s were to be concerned with children suffering "any disability of mind and body", and special schools were regarded as necessary.

Endeavours were made continuously to provide an effective system of further education, and as has been shown this was proposed in the 1944 Act. The Hadow Report of 1926 considered that teachers in senior schools should draw attention to facilities for further education in their areas both cultural and vocational. The system of compulsory day release which had not been realized after 1918 was a subject for pessimism, and in 1938 there were only 51,000 such students.

The scene was set in 1944 for a raising of the level of literacy to higher peaks than ever before. The extent to which each individual progressed, however, was related not so much to the expansion of educational opportunities, but among other factors, to the methods which were applied in the schools at the various levels, and which must be geared to the capacity and aptitude of the individual.

The importance of reading was stressed in all the reports from Newbolt to Spens. In 1921 children were not, as a rule, sufficiently encouraged to use books for information, but in instances where textbooks were superseded by information books, children were given the opportunity to acquire knowledge for themselves. "Above all", said Newbolt, "the children should discover the delight of books". It was not sufficient, however, to read a number of books, unless the habit of reading for pleasure and information was formed. Children should be trained not only to appreciate good general literature but also to read books relating to such subjects as engineering, gardening, housecraft, physical exercises and games (Hadow, 1926). It may not be possible to create in all children a love of literature, but it was of practical advantage to teach all of them to use books (Hadow, 1928).

Welsh education was considered in the latter report and a primary defect was found to be the lack of suitable books. Publishers had difficulty in producing books in Welsh due to the limited demand, although there had been a steady improvement since 1918. A report on *Welsh in Education and Life* (1927) recommended that:

1. The University Press Board should act as adviser to publishers and encourage authors to write books in Welsh for children.
2. Each L.E.A. should maintain a collection of text and reading books in Welsh for inspection by teachers and parents.
3. Welsh books should be provided in school libraries.
4. A supplementary allowance should be made by each L.E.A. for the provision of books for the teaching of Welsh.

The Hadow Committee (1928) supported the proposals and called for more generous grants for books in public elementary schools in Wales.

The older ideas that education implied instruction from books had been replaced by a wider interpretation, and the project and activity methods had modified the proportion of time devoted to their use. No reference was made to books in the Code of 1926 in contrast to those of 1906 and 1907 which have been discussed. Several witnesses before the Hadow Committee (1926) criticized courses through which children were led to talk about things "instead of doing them". It was admitted in the Hadow Report of 1928 that "Books, it is true, are not the only instrument of education, or the sole avenue to the world of culture". Even in 1928 it was possible to discover schools in which the tradition of three reading books had survived, in many the oral lesson continued to be regarded as the most important means of instruction, and except in the reading lesson the book played a minor part.

It is of interest to study the methods and ideas which were prevalent in the teaching of reading. The child was to begin to learn the three R's when he wished to do so whether he was 3 or 6 years old. Whatever method was used (Look and Say, Phonics, or the more recent Sentence method) the ability to read could only be acquired by a great deal of practice, and a problem for the teacher was to devise a means for making available this facility. Classes were frequently divided into small groups for the reading lesson and given sufficient practice so that on transfer to the junior school children could be expected to read for pleasure. In the Hadow Report of 1933 it was suggested that the first step was to secure word recognition, but by 1937 it was regarded as essential that children should be taught "to make the phrase and not the word the unit of reading". In 1937 it was considered "wisest with the majority of children to postpone formal instruction" in the three R's until they were approximately 6 years old. Reading primers in use between the wars included *Beacon Readers* (1922), *The Land of Sunshine* (1931), *Radiant Way Readers* (1933), *Holloway Readers* (1935), *John and Mary Readers* (1937), and *The Happy Venture Readers* (1939).

An adequate supply of books was to be kept in classrooms in elementary schools for purposes of reference and home reading. The books would mainly consist of stories in the cases of younger children on the subjects of aircraft, exploration and nature study, and in addition to the enjoyment of reading, children would increase their vocabularies and phraseology (Hadow, 1931). There was a particular need for a wide variety of books in schools where individual methods had been adopted, a requirement which was so often at variance with the reality, for not only did the supply of books require to be increased but the quality frequently was poor. "In the country as a whole the situation was often serious and sometimes deplorable" (Hadow, 1928), and yet in the 1930's "a better and more varied choice of books" was being published "than at any previous time" (Suggestions, 1937).

Children were to be trained in the use of books so that they would refer to them instead of relying for all their information on teachers. Unless the habit of consulting books for information became automatic it could not be claimed that children had been taught to read. It was important for children to learn to use indexes and tables of contents, and to identify abbreviations and signs in common use. Thus equipped they would be able to obtain information more rapidly. This kind of activity was regarded as quite as useful in the junior as in the senior school.

Numerous books were to be read in the senior school and teachers could compile lists of material to facilitate such a programme. It was necessary not only to read for information but also

> ... for some familiarity with the experience which finds expression in literature, for imaginative contact with the lives of others, for the acquisition of a set of values which will stand him in good stead in the world of books and in the wider world in which his life must be lived, and incidentally for the enjoyment of what is well written. [Suggestions, 1937.]

In the highest classes children were to have access to books containing "vivid descriptions of places, peoples, animal and vegetable life" which would supplement oral teaching, such as R. Finch's *Geography through the Shop Window* (Evans, 1931), W. B. Little's *Science in the City* (Pitman, 1931) and *Science in the Home* (Pitman, 1935), E. Young's *At Work in Many Lands* (Evans, 1933), G. Blake's *British Ships and Shipbuilders* (Collins, 1938), and the Petershams' *The Story Book of Cotton* (Wells, Gardner, 1939) and other volumes in the same series.

A stock of well-chosen reference books was essential, such as *Whitaker's Almanack*, Ordnance Survey maps, official statistical reports, all of which it was sometimes possible to borrow from the public library. In science there were many simple books which could assist in the identification of common plants, insects and natural phenomena, including Andrade and Huxley's *Forces At Work* (Blackwell, 1934), and T. J. S. Rowland's *Burning and Breathing* (Cassell, 1938). In the immediate years before the 1944 Act, Collins published the outstanding *Book of Wild Flowers* (1943) and *Book of Birds* (1944) by Richard Morse.

After 1918 the books for use in schools became more attractive in appearance, and more interesting. Much of the improvement in presentation was thought to derive from the British Association report in 1913 relating to *The Influence of School Books upon Eyesight*, in which sizes of type were specified for children of particular ages. Improvements were also due to standards which were set by the L.C.C. and other L.E.A.s regarding the appearance and type of school books, and the lists which they compiled for the guidance of teachers. Criticisms, however, could be levelled at many books which were too large to be comfortably handled by younger children, and in which the illustrations were unnecessarily elaborate, features which entailed increased prices. Frequently the illustrations were placed unsuitably in relation to the text they were "intended to elucidate" (Hadow, 1928).

Books were available relating to all manner of practical subjects: knitting, needlework, weaving, metal work and woodwork, and various hobbies. Examples included A. C. Horth's *101 Things for a Boy to Make* (Batsford, 1928), and *101 Things for a Girl to Make* (Batsford, 1935), and *Beaten Metal Work* (Pitman, 1930), D. P. Harding's *Glove Puppetry For Young Children* (Blackwell, 1938), and M. Tillotson's *The Complete Knitting Book* (Pitman, 1940).

The Spens Committee (1938) discussed the use of books in the secondary school, and drew attention to the emotional appeal to teenagers of English literature:

> Love of reading, joy in the discovery of literary beauty, enlargement of imaginative experience, these are among the most treasured fruits of a sound English education.

It was felt that the study of prescribed books for examinations was detrimental to the growth of interest in literature, and recommended without success that this practice should be discontinued.

Young people were to read books of their own choice with no tutorial censorship, but a tactful raising of the standard "by comment and encouragement". If the teacher revealed his own pleasure in a book, the imitative nature of the pupils would impel them to try and share in the experience. The practice of reading passages of prose or poetry without comment was suggested, and "in short a good teacher could do almost anything to induce a love of reading except teach it".

Before 1920 the house of Dent was known principally for its school books in modern languages, but in that year published the first 25 volumes in its *Kings' Treasuries of Literature* series. The aim was to produce a book which would by its very appearance enhance the appeal of English literature to the pupil. By 1938 there were 251 volumes in this series, edited through the years by Sir Arthur Quiller Couch, and later by Guy Pocock. John Drinkwater edited a number of reading books and a series of single plays of Shakespeare for Collins, and his anthology *The Way of Poetry* enjoyed great popularity.

Various publishers made their contribution to secondary education. After 1918, Collins discarded many of their old texts and replaced them with a series of specially commissioned works by experts such as Kenneth Bell the historian, T. W. F. Parkinson, and Dr. Marion Newbiggin, both eminent geographers.

In 1927 Dent planned a series of science books and in 1928 Dr. Eric Holmyard accepted the position of editor. Early examples of his work in the *Modern Science Series* were *Chemistry for Beginners* (1930) and *Physics for Beginners* (1930). Interest was shown by the firm in history when G. W. Southgate's *A Textbook of Modern English History* was published in 1932, and which was followed in 1934 with *English Economic History* by the same author. Another outstanding writer for Dent was Thomas Pickles, whose *A Revision Course in Geography* (1931) was factual and extremely readable. In 1938 Dent was responsible for a wide range of school books.

Disquiet was shown by the Spens Committee as regards the reading habits of science pupils, and an extract (quoted earlier) was included from the publication *Natural Science in Education* with the codicil:

> We would remind science teachers of these remarks and would affirm our belief that they afford a warning that is still necessary.

The examination system which pervaded (and pervades) the selective secondary school resulted in an unbalanced preoccupation with textbooks in arts subjects, together with their relegation to the role of ancillaries in the sciences, whilst general reading was not sufficiently encouraged in either case.

The position of books in evening schools was discussed by the Newbolt Committee where it was revealed that students not only resented lessons in English but did their utmost to avoid them. It was considered that English should somehow be related to students' vocations and this was accomplished by widening the definition of the subject to include a study of the geography and history of particular industries in the locality of schools. Thus a textbook of social history was substituted for novels as a basis for class-work in English. In instances where the experiment was attempted, the popularity of English was increased.

As regards the proposed day continuation schools the Newbolt Committee declared that there were boundless possibilities for the creation of readers who had "hitherto left school too early to acquire the habit". It was not then realized that the concept of the day continuation school was not to be realized at that time, but the principle of the Committee's claim remains constant. Collins actually planned a series of books for the proposed schools, which included a book on economics by Mrs. Lettice Fisher (wife of H. A. L. Fisher), and histories by Professor Raymond Beazley and Andrew Browning.

The adequacy of books in schools was dependent of course on the financial provision made by the L.E.A.s. The most common method was the adoption of a scale of capitation allowances which was varied to meet the special needs of different types of school. Sometimes, however, the grants were fixed, which did not allow for the needs of small schools, advanced classes, or for instances where new methods were introduced, but frequently, supplementary payments were made in these circumstances. The Hadow Committee (1928) advocated the imposition of a fixed scale of grants for books, stationery and apparatus, with a special fund for particular requirements.

Twenty-three L.E.A.s furnished the Hadow Committee with information regarding their expenditure. In these areas the average annual sum per pupil which was spent between 1924 and 1927 was 2s. 9d. in senior schools, 1s. 9d. in junior schools, 6s. 8d. in infant schools, and 1s. 9d. in small schools. Statistics supplied by the Board of Education showed that the gross expenditure on books and stationery in elementary schools in England and Wales in 1925/6 was 5s. 7d. per pupil, a sum which represented less than 1% of the total *per capita* expenditure in these schools. Authorities which neither applied the *per capita* nor the fixed allowances included Liverpool, Plymouth, and Middlesex.

The improved supply of new books, however, was not solely a matter of expenditure but of careful selection by teachers. Permanent book rooms provided by such L.E.A.s as Manchester, and the counties of Cardigan, Kent, Lincoln, and Middlesex, were very useful. Booklists were compiled for the guidance of teachers by the L.C.C., Liverpool, and Kent, the latter of which was first published in 1922, and supplemented in 1925 and also in *The Kent Education Gazette*. Other aids to book selection were the exhibitions which were often set up at teachers' courses, advice from H.M.I.s, public libraries, and publishers' representatives, and the scrutiny of new books forwarded from publishers. The formation of the National Book Council (1925) which became the National Book League in 1944; the School Library Association in 1937; and the Schools Section of the Library Association also in 1937, was to exercise a positive influence in the provision of books in schools, as will be demonstrated in a later chapter.

It is apparent that the growth of literacy was encouraged by a number of factors between 1918 and 1939 but the results of the wartime evacuation proved overwhelmingly retrogressive. There were rumours that many children lost their ability to read due to lack of practice. Evidence was gathered in Kent among other areas to show that the war had a detrimental effect on standards of reading and although improvements took place in the post-war years, the level which obtained in 1939 was not re-established. It is surely a tragedy that the endeavours of generations should have been so easily undermined.

CHAPTER 17

Mediocrity and Escapism in Children's Literature   1920–1945

THE rise in the price of new books after World War I resulted in the issue by publishers of large numbers of mass produced rewards which were printed on featherweight paper (70% air) to give the illusion of value in bulk. Annuals and bumper books were also prolific. They cost 1s. 6d. to 2s. 6d. and contained, between garish covers, short stories, poems, and articles, interspersed with indifferent illustrations. Reprints of 19th-century adventure and girls' stories were also popular. In fact more books were published than ever before, most of them of poor quality both physically and in their contents.

Lionel McColvin, a well-known librarian, in his column in *The Library Association Record* in 1932 referred to the availability of

> a few admirable books . . . submerged in an ocean of terrible trash—unreal school stories, impossible adventures, half-witted fairy tales and footling poetry; books written by hacks, slovenly, often ignorantly; books full of sentimentality and humbug; books which . . . promote a wrong sense of values . . . And the production equals the matter. In every respect—paper, binding, printing, illustrations—most of these juvenile books are disgraceful.

Marcus Crouch has pointed out that the depression of the 1930's influenced publishing trends later than other sectors of the economy, and apart from an increase in the years 1936 and 1937, there was a decline in the number of new children's books:

1934	1490	1937	1597
1935	1345	1938	1406
1936	1540	1939	1303

However, there was no reflection in children's books of the economic difficulties. The mood of the 1930's was one of escapism on both the national and international scenes. In children's literature the dream was purveyed through fantasy, whether at school, at home, or in some unrealistic adventurous setting. The impact of cinema and radio meant that children could not only read this kind of literature but also see and hear it.

The possibilities of improvement in the quality of children's publishing emerged with the appointment of children's editors, as for example Miss M. C. Carey at Dent's in 1936, and Mary Treadgold at Heinemann's in 1939. An increased interest was also evident in the publication of F. J. Harvey Darton's *Children's Books in England* in 1932; the appearance of the reviewing periodical *Junior Bookshelf* in 1936; the inauguration of the Library Association's Carnegie Medal, which in 1937 was awarded to the outstanding British children's book of 1936; and A. J. Jenkinson's survey *What Do Boys and Girls Read?* in 1940.

In the 1920's, adventure stories were represented by the work of Harry Collingwood, Captain W. E. Johns, and Percy Westerman; there were also books involving the exploits of scouts and guides by such writers as Vera Barclay and John Finnemore; and Richmal Crompton's famous *Just William* introduced himself in 1922. The following decades, however, witnessed a big improvement in quality in the books of Arthur Ransome; and the domestically centred contributions of Pamela Brown, Eve Garnett, Eleanor Graham, and Noel Streatfeild, the latter being responsible for a number of outstanding career novels. Ransome depicted a middle-class children's paradise in the tradition of Jefferies and Seton, and was himself imitated in *The Far Distant Oxus* by Katharine Hull and Pamela Whitlock; whilst Eve Garnett wrote of working-class people without resorting to caricature.

There was also a constant interest in historical stories, but these were mainly adventure stories in a historical setting. It was the adventure theme in which the interest lay, in the romances of Herbert Strang and others. Once more, however, the quality improved in the 1930's with C. Walter Hodges' *Columbus Sails*

(1939), Carola Oman's *Robin Hood* (1939), Geoffrey Trease's *Bows against the Barons* (1934), and Alison Uttley's *A Traveller in Time* (1939).

School stories were very popular between the wars. Those for boys were written by E. F. Benson, Richard Bird, Hylton Cleaver and Gunby Hadath; and for girls by Angela Brazil, Eleanor Brent-Dyer, Winifred Darch, Josephine Elder, and Elsie Oxenham. Many of these books were more concerned with the relationships of the characters than with school activities. This was also true of the so-called pony stories of Joanna Cannan, Allen Chaffee, "Golden Gorse", Primrose Cumming, Ann Stafford, and Mary Treadgold, which were more concerned with the social aspects than with technical details.

Most of the books mentioned in this chapter so far were fanciful in their own way. Even Eve Garnett's family was far removed from the dole queues and the means test of the depression. In the more specific field of what is normally thought of as fantasy, the contributors were often outstanding and included Walter de la Mare, Eleanor Farjeon, Hilda Lewis, John Masefield, Geoffrey Mure, J. R. R. Tolkien, Alison Uttley, and during the war, Eric Linklater, Mary Norton and D. J. Watkins-Pitchford. Attention was also given to fairy tales. A large number of editions of Hans Andersen's tales was published after 1920. Walter de la Mare's *Told Again* (1927) consisted of traditional fairy tales.

Animal fantasies were well represented and the only outstanding author in any category of fiction who made his first appearance in the 1920's was A. A. Milne, creator of *Winnie the Pooh* (1926). His animals were mainly toys as were those of Margery Bianco and Ursula Moray Williams. Real animals in stories of fantasy were created by Patricia Lynch and Alison Uttley, and in 1929 Beatrix Potter's less successful *Fairy Caravan* was published.

A high quality of poetry was available in de la Mare's *Down-a-Down-Derry* (1922) and in his *Poems for Children* (1930); in A. A. Milne's *When We Were Very Young* (1924) (Fig. 22) and *Now We Are Six* (1927); and in Eleanor Farjeon's *Over the Garden Wall* (1933), *Sing for your Supper* (1938), and *Cherry*

WHEN WE WERE VERY YOUNG BY A. A. MILNE WITH DECORATIONS BY ERNEST H. SHEPARD

METHUEN & CO. LTD. 36 ESSEX STREET
LONDON W.C.

Thirteenth Edition

FIG. 22. Title page from A. A. Milne's *When We Were Very Young*. 1924. (By courtesy of Methuen & Co. Ltd.)

Stones (1942). Outstanding anthologies included de la Mare's *Come Hither* (1923) and *Tom Tiddler's Ground* (1932), and W. H. Auden's and J. Garrett's compilation *Poet's Tongue* (1935), which David Holbrook has judged to be "the best in existence".

Attractive picture books were produced and immortal characters were born on the drawing boards of Edward Ardizzone (Little Tim), V. H. Drummond (Mrs. Easter), and Kathleen Hale (Orlando the Marmalade Cat). In the autumn of 1936, Dent published a picture book entitled *The Little Boy and his House* which was written and illustrated by Stephen Bone and Mary Adshead. Other experiments in colour lithography were made in the Petersham's series of books on a variety of commodities; and the first Puffin Picture Books edited by Noel Carrington which appeared from 1940 and included *Village and Town* (1942) and *Trees in Britain* (1943).

Successful illustrators in the 1920's and 1930's included C. Walter Hodges and E. H. Shepard, who worked mainly in black and white, a style which presented a contrast with the earlier ornately colourful productions of Dulac and Rackham. Other illustrators associated with children's books in the period included S. G. Hulme Beaman, F. D. Bedford, Charles Folkard, Rowland Hilder, Robert Gibbings, Gwen Raverat, and Rex Whistler, the scraperboard work of whose edition of Andersen being particularly pleasing. It was also in these years that the dust jacket emerged as a means of drawing the interest of children and also as a means of advertising other titles in the same series or by the same author.

Non-fiction became increasingly attractive and interesting, and in view of the activity methods adopted in schools, there ceased to be any definite distinction between books for home reading and for use in school. It would be impossible to do full justice to the many works which appeared, but there was a wide coverage of subjects for the various ages.

Outstanding examples in science included J. H. Fabre's *The Life of Spiders* (Hodder, 1927), Amabel Williams-Ellis' *Men who Found Out* (Bodley Head, 1929), Willi Gail's *Romping through*

Physics (Routledge, 1933), Sir Laurence Bragg's *Electricity* (Bell, 1936), Eleanor Doorly's *Radium Woman* (Heinemann, 1939), and for younger children, Lida's *Frou the Hare* (Allen & Unwin) and others in the same series.

In history may be cited H. E. Marshall's *Our Island Story* (Nelson, 1920), D. M. Stuart's *The Boy through the Ages* (Harrap, 1926), Eileen and Rhoda Power's *Boys and Girls of History* (Cambridge, 1926), M. B. Synge's *A Book of Discovery* (Nelson, 1929), the Quennells' *Everyday Life in Ancient Greece* (Batsford, 1929), R. N. D. Wilson's *Early Man* (Jack, 1933), and Eleanor Doorly's *The Story of France* (Cape, 1944).

Other books of the period which spring to mind are Ana M. Berry's *Art for Children* (Studio, 1929), Ernest La Prade's *Alice in Orchestraland* (Bodley, 1934), Freda Holmdahl's *The Rainy Day Book* (Nelson, 1936), Opal Wheeler and Sybil Deucher's *Mozart the Wonder Boy* (Faber, 1939), and Lucy Diamond's *How the Gospel Came to Britain* (O.U.P., 1944). Dent's *Everyday Series*, written by M. C. Carey and illustrated by Mary Shillabeer and Nora Lavrin, were a major contribution to the "here and now" world of younger children in such titles as *The Milkman* and *The Policeman* (1938).

Reference books became more common, examples of which were Cassell's *Children's Book of Knowledge*, in 7 volumes (1924/6), Harry Golding's *The Wonder Book of Do You Know?* (Ward Lock, 1934), and Newnes' *Pictorial Knowledge*, in 8 volumes (1930/5). Dictionaries were represented by Harold Wheeler's *The Waverley Children's Dictionary*, in 8 volumes (1929), and Arthur Mee's *The Pictorial Dictionary*, in 5 volumes (Educational Book Co., 1930), but most of the reference books were standard works and not specially compiled for children.

More material was imported from the United States where in the 1920's there was a great deal of activity in the field of children's books. The interest was symbolized in the institution of the Newbery Medal from 1922, the appearance of *The Horn Book Magazine* (1924), the publication of Mahoney and Whitney's *Realms of Gold in Children's Books* (1929), and the formation of the Young People's Reading Round Table (1929). Outstanding writers of children's books were Elizabeth Enright, Eleanor Estes, Charles Finger, Esther Forbes, Wanda Gág, Elizabeth Janet Gray, Hugh Lofting, D. G. Mukerji, and Armstrong Sperry. Particularly outstanding were the American picture books which were of a far higher standard than the equivalent British productions in the 1930's. Among the finest picture books issued in British editions were Maud and Miska Petersham's *The Christ Child* (1933), Marjorie Flack's *Angus and the Ducks* (1933), Wanda Gág's *Snow White and the Seven Dwarfs* (1938) and Willie Pogany's *The Golden Cockerell* (1939).

Some examples of European literature were translated and published in British editions, but between 1933 and 1945 only 100 such books were dealt with in this manner, there being a peak of 18 in 1936 but only 2 in 1933 and never more than 7 in any year during the war. From France, Jean de Brunhoff's *The Story of Babar*, was first translated in 1934, and Antoine St. Exupéry's *The Little Prince* in 1945. Other notable writers were Erich Kästner of Germany and H. J. Kaeser of Sweden, whose boy characters Emil and Mimff were introduced to British children in 1931 and 1939 respectively.

Book prices remained beyond the resources of the majority of children. The economic situation which resulted in the unemployment of so many parents curtailed the amount of money which could be spent on books, and editions were not available in paper covers until after 1940. Production costs rose quickly after World War I to three times the level at which they had stood in 1914. Adult novels which had sold at 6s. were forced up to 7s. in the autumn of 1919, and to 9s. in 1920. Children's books after 1920 cost approximately 7s. 6d., the initial price of Milne's *When We Were Very Young* (1924), Masefield's *The Midnight Folk* (1927), Ransome's *Swallows and Amazons* (1930) (Fig. 23) and Tolkien's *The Hobbit* (1937). Books which were cheaper included Crompton's *Just William* (1922), Trease's *Bows against the Barons* (1934), and Garnett's *The Family From One-End Street* (1937), which ranged from 2s. 6d. to 5s. Picture books ranged from 2s. 6d. for Wanda

Swallows & Amazons

by

Arthur Ransome

SWALLOWS·AND·AMAZONS·FOR·EVER!

Illustrated by the Author
with help from Miss Nancy Blackett

London

Jonathan Cape, Thirty Bedford Square

FIG. 23. Title page from Arthur Ransome's *Swallows and Amazons.* 1930. (By courtesy of Jonathan Cape Ltd.)

Gág's *Millions of Cats* (1929) to 7s. 6d. for Ardizzone's *Little Tim and the Brave Sea Captain* (1936).

There was, said L. R. McColvin in 1932, a need for a detailed survey of children's reading. He considered it important that the relationship between reading for adults and children should be more clearly understood, and the themes, treatment, and literary style in relation to taste and development should be investigated. Surveys of some interest were made at this time in Derbyshire in 1932 and East Ham in 1934, but the most detailed, A. J. Jenkinson's *What Do Boys and Girls Read?*, was published in 1940. This was compiled from a questionnaire which was sent to 17 senior and 11 secondary schools. Although replies were not received from 50%, approximately 3000 answers were obtained from boys and girls aged 12–15 years. It was discovered that the most popular class of reading among boys was the adventure story, whilst with girls the most popular books were those about home and school. Boys of 12 preferred school stories after adventure, but as they grew older they became interested in detective and historical tales. A popular writer for boys was Richmal Crompton, the author of the *William* books. Girls favoured L. M. Alcott, Susan Coolidge, and L. M. Montgomery, and gave some attention to love stories. Other points which emerged from the survey were that girls read more than boys at all ages, not only novels, but plays, poetry and essays.

Many young people were aware of adult authors, some of whom they would read in school such as the Brontës and Dickens. In addition, however, many claimed to have read books by John Buchan and P. G. Wodehouse, and there can be no doubt that other adopted literature of an earlier generation would have its place in their leisure pursuits. Secondary school pupils could often be expected to read adult literature when they had outgrown children's books, but there was a definite gap in the provision made for the less intellectual sections of the adolescent community who would be likely to resort to periodicals of various descriptions.

The outstanding periodical for younger children published in these years was Basil Blackwell's *Merry Go Round* (1923/39) which was issued monthly and edited by Rose Fyleman. *The B.O.P.*, *The G.O.P.*, Mee's *Children's Newspaper*, and *My Magazine*, continued to appear, but the latter ceased publication in 1933, whilst the long lived *Little Folks* was discontinued in 1931.

In the world of the comic Harmsworth's Amalgamated Press enjoyed a monopoly from 1890 until the 1930's. Among 40 or more papers were *Film Fun*, *Girls' Crystal*, and *Playbox*. Towards the end of the 1930's the Scottish firm of D. C. Thomson Ltd. began to compete with *Dandy* (1937), *Beano* (1938) and *Magic* (1939), the latter being suspended during the war and never revived. Thomson was responsible for the introduction of rhyming captions, which were not used by Harmsworth. Another popular periodical was Odham's *Mickey Mouse* (1936).

Many of the comics were also issued in annual form, the familiar characters taking part in a number of new but trivial incidents, either pictorially or in stories. An outstanding annual which was not in the same category as most of the others was Basil Blackwell's *Joy Street*, which was published regularly from 1923 to 1936. The distinguished list of contributors included Hilaire Belloc, G. K. Chesterton, Walter de la Mare, Eleanor Farjeon, Laurence Housman, Compton Mackenzie, A. A. Milne, and Edith Sitwell. The emphasis in this as in other periodicals was placed on fantasy, which was, as has been shown, in conformity with the spirit of the era.

Jenkinson discovered in 1940 that the favourite periodicals of teenage boys were *John Bull*, *Passing Show*, *Everybody's* and *Hobbies*, whilst girls preferred the first three and *Picturegoer* rather than *Hobbies*. Newspapers were read too, but their choice was determined by that of parents: *Daily Express*, *Daily Herald*, *Daily Mail*, *Daily Telegraph*, and a variety of local journals. Many teenagers read the non-pictorial comics of Harmsworth and Thomson such as *Adventure*, *Champion*, *Hotspur*, *Rover*, *Skipper*, and *Wizard*, which contained stories of adventure, school, and sport, with the addition of military and secret service exploits during the war years.

The impact of World War II has been described as it affected the educational system, and it also almost destroyed the publishing trade. Schools were requisitioned for government purposes, and among other publishers, Blackie arranged to use 33% of their factory space in the manufacture of shells for the Ministry of Supply. The first labour force in the new factory in 1941 was comprised of Blackie's employees.

Withdrawal of labour for military service and factory employment, and the requisition of space for the manufacture of armaments was only a part of the story. As a result of enemy action, British publishers lost 20 million books, and when Paternoster Row was destroyed in the bombing of one night, 6 million books were burned. Cassell's lost 480 tons of bound and unbound stock representing nearly $1\frac{1}{2}$ million volumes. Paternoster Row was the home of English publishing, and involved in the destruction were the houses of Bagster, Longman, Nelson, Sheed & Ward, and Simpkin-Marshall.

A combination of circumstances, therefore, including a shortage of materials resulted in a sharp reduction in the publication of new books for children:

1940	973	1943	671
1941	520	1944	785
1942	595	1945	715

Not until 1948 was the total to exceed 1000. After the war, the reward trade never recovered owing to the destruction of 1940/41. The standard of children's books was generally poor in wartime, and on two occasions the Carnegie Medal was not awarded.

Children's books reflected the period in which they were written to an extent which had not been so since World War I. Two Carnegie awards were relevant to the hostilities: Kitty Barne's *Visitors From London* (1940) was concerned with the evacuation, and Mary Treadgold's *We Could'nt Leave Dinah* (1941) described the German invasion of the Channel Islands. Kitty Barne wrote *In the Same Boat* (1945), Lorna Lewis, *Tea and Hot Bombs* (1943), Richmal Crompton, *William and A.R.P.* (Air Raid Precautions)

(1939) and *William and the Evacuees* (1940), and W. E. Johns, the adventures of Biggles and Worralls, most of which were "produced in complete conformity with the authorized economy standards". The most prolific and most popular author of the war years was Enid Blyton, whose work has been widely and often unfairly criticized.

During the war the weekly comics were withdrawn in some instances such as *Magic* and *Skipper*, but in others, such as *Beano* and *Dandy*, and *Adventure* and *Wizard*, they were issued on alternate weeks in a substantially reduced form. In these years a comic starved juvenile population was exposed to American publications which were introduced by U.S. servicemen. These papers included "funnies", which were originally inserts in the American press, but many were so horrific in content that a post-war generation was to attempt to have them banned with mixed success.

The war was helpful to children's literature in that much of the dross was purged and the opportunity given for a resurgence which was to herald a Second Golden Age. However, the level of literacy did not keep pace with the improved literary standards, and as in the past, better quality children's books were the preserve of a minority, whilst the majority still monopolized the descendants of penny dreadfuls and other trivia of the 19th century.

CHAPTER 18

Libraries for Children
1919–1945

THE value of libraries in schools was the subject of continuous comment in the numerous reports issued by the Board of Education, both in those which were concerned with the educational system, such as the Consultative Committees, and also in the Kenyon Report on *The Public Library Service* (1927). The latter Committee was "strongly of the opinion that every school, elementary or secondary should have a well equipped library in proportion to its needs".

A number of publications appeared, including Marjorie Peacock's *A School and Club Librarians' Handbook* (1920), which was "intended for the guidance of amateur or untrained librarians in schools"; Ethel Fegan's *School Libraries* (1928); L. S. Jast's *The Provision of Books for Children in Elementary Schools* (1928), the Carnegie United Kingdom Trust's *Libraries in Secondary Schools* (1936), and the Association of Assistant Masters' *Guide for School Librarians* (1937). From 1935 to 1939, the Board of Education sponsored short courses in school librarianship.

The formation of the School Library Association, and the Schools Section of the Library Association in 1937 acted as catalysts. The S.L.A. was founded to promote the development and use of the school library as an instrument of education in schools of all kinds, and to this end, organized branches, published booklists, pamphlets, and its mouthpiece *The School Librarian* (1937); whilst the Schools Section of the L.A. had similar aims and functions and publicized its views in *The School Library Review* (1936). In the early years of World War II the S.L.A. set up a committee to report and make recommendations on the provision of libraries in grammar schools, and the findings were published in *The School Librarian* in December 1942 and in pamphlet form in 1943. A joint committee of the S.L.A. and the Schools Section of the L.A. was set up in 1943 to consider the provision of libraries in elementary schools, but owing to the passage of the 1944 Act the report eventually emerged as a statement of the need for school libraries in general. It was published in 1945 under the title *School Libraries in Post-War Reconstruction: a joint report*. As a practical gesture the Schools Section of the L.A. agreed to become part of the S.L.A. in 1946.

Particular assistance was rendered to school librarians by the publication of booklists after 1937. The S.L.A.'s publications included *General Reference Books* (1939) and various subject lists compiled in collaboration with interested organizations. For example, *Domestic Subjects* (1938) was produced with the Association of Teachers of Domestic Subjects, and *Scripture* (1938) with the Institute of Christian Education. Schools Section lists were included in *The School Library Review* among which were *The Arts Section* (1941) and *Birds* (1942/3).

The Kenyon Report of 1927 expressed the view that local education committees should be responsible for the provision of school libraries, which should receive grants from the Board of Education. The Hadow Committee on *Books in Public Elementary Schools* (1928) was in agreement with this view. In practice school libraries were gradually built up from the general allowance for books and stationery, and in many instances were maintained almost entirely by voluntary means. Several L.E.A.s gave grants at the inception of libraries, whilst others made separate annual allowances.

In the elementary schools the consensus of opinion was that classroom collections were more appropriate than central school libraries. Hadow (1928) considered that the choice should be made by head teachers, but in the report on *The Primary School* (1931) the witnesses "were, on the whole, of opinion that in the larger primary schools class libraries were preferable . . . ". The

Hadow Report on *The Education of the Adolescent* (1926) advocated class libraries, but this opinion was radically modified in later years as will be demonstrated later in this chapter.

The necessity for providing suitable shelves and a systematic arrangement of the books was emphasized (Hadow, 1928), and the Board's *Suggestions for the Planning of Buildings for Public Elementary Schools* (1937) listed the main requirements as adequate lighting, and bookshelves designed so that the children could see and choose books for themselves.

Collections were to consist of story books "if the pupils were to be encouraged to read as copiously as was desirable", but it was also important to cater for the numerous children who were interested in plants and animals, aeroplanes, ships, steam engines and railways, motor cars, photography, wireless telegraphy, games, arts and crafts, and other subjects. Books of reference were also to be included. New trends were manifest in the desirability of choosing books "not designed by their authors for use as school books" (*Suggestions for Teachers*, 1937). It was necessary for the children to receive instruction in the use of the library so that they would "more readily appreciate the value of the public library" (Hadow, 1928).

For older children "the balance and range of the books should be such as to include historical novels and biographies, books of travel, English classics and good anthologies of English verse" (Hadow, 1926). The books could well be arranged in class libraries but there should also be a general school library if possible, containing standard works of reference and books about the locality. The science section was to include suitable books on British and local geology, flora and fauna, and, subject to local circumstances, material on sea fisheries or coalmining. Biographies of great scientists were an additional advantage. Musical compositions and histories and biographies of music and musicians to be used by the pupils were also recommended.

In 1937 very few schools were able to place their books in a special room where the atmosphere was conducive both to "serious study and recreative reading". It was, however, recognized as desirable that the senior school should possess a library.

Secondary school library facilities were regarded as at their most useful when centralized. Where activity methods were used in elementary schools a collection of books was needed where the work was taking place, that is in the classroom, and it was also conducive to the formation of reading habits if the books were immediately to hand. However, secondary school subjects were taught in rigid disciplines, and as these overlapped, the most practical solution was to have one collection. This idea was supported by those responsible for the Board's Memorandum on *Libraries in State Aided Secondary Schools* (1928), the Board's *Secondary School Buildings Pamphlet* (1931), the Carnegie United Kingdom Trust's *Libraries in Secondary Schools* (1936), and the Spens (1938) and Norwood (1943) Reports.

The approach to classroom collections in secondary schools varied. If it was impossible to provide accommodation for a separate building, the Memorandum of 1928 advocated that shelves and furniture should be suitable for transfer to a library at a later date, but whatever the situation "the whole supply of books which the school possesses should be regarded as the school library". Free access to the books was important and could not be effective when classrooms housing collections were in use for tutorial purposes. The Carnegie Report was opposed to class libraries unless there were no other facilities, whilst the Spens Committee regarded small class libraries as "often an additional help".

The first priority was books, stated the Memorandum of 1928, and listed the minimum book requirements of every secondary school by subjects. Similar suggestions were made by the C.U.K.T. report. Ideally, however, the library should not simply contain books but also comfortable chairs (Spens), and Carnegie specified requirements regarding accommodation and equipment.

The Norwood Report stressed the need for training in the correct use of books, and the encouragement of pupils to read background material. This could only be satisfactorily accomplished if the staff included a master who had undergone some training in librarianship, an experience which was possible after 1935 through the useful courses organized by the Board of Education. Very few schools were likely to require a full-time librarian, although the circumstances of particular schools might justify such a step (Carnegie). Whoever was chosen to organize the library should be "a lover of books, he must be an educationist in the broadest sense of that word, and must possess the abilities of an administrator" (Carnegie). The Spens and Norwood Committees both envisaged someone to help and advise pupils, but neither thought in terms other than "a teacher acting as librarian".

As regards provision in institutions devoted to further education, the Newbolt Committee on *The Teaching of English in England* (1921) recommended "a good library . . . both for use and for delight". However, the facilities did not show improvement in the following decades, and in a report on *Policy in Technical Education* in 1937 by the Association of Teachers in Technical Institutions, the absence of library facilities was strongly criticized.

Progress in public libraries was slow. The Hadow Committee (1928) commended:

> the practice now obtaining in many public libraries of reserving special rooms, or portions of rooms, as reading rooms for children . . . All public library committees should, where possible, organize juvenile lending departments. The children should if possible be allowed personal access to the bookshelves in the juvenile department.

It was also regarded as necessary for areas which had not adopted the Public Libraries Act to do so either singly or in combination.

At that time library work with children was in the process of expansion, but on the whole it was not intensive. Economic difficulties were a hindrance to development, but there was also an absence of interest.

Concern was felt in the 1930's regarding children's work. No articles appeared on the subject in the Library Association's *The Year's Work in Librarianship* between 1929 and 1936. In the latter year the Westminster Public Library reported a reduction in the use made of facilities by children as a result of which it was proposed to discontinue the work in this field. Various factors were held responsible for the depressing situation including the increase in the number of school libraries, a fall in the birthrate, and the popularity of the cinema.

However, in 1937 the picture appeared to improve and reports on increases in the issues of children's books were widespread. In this year an Association of Children's Librarians was formed, which superseded an earlier Circle of Library Workers with Children (1933). The concept of an organization of this kind was crystallized at the Library Association Conference at Harrogate in 1933. It was proposed initially that the children's librarians should form a section of the Library Association, but this was opposed and for many years the new group remained an independent body. A number of new libraries were opened during 1938, and in almost all of them, provision was made for children.

It is relevant to comment on unfortunate attitudes to children which prevailed among numerous librarians. Perhaps this was typified by an address to the Library Association Conference in 1933 when a lady delegate invited her audience to thank God for the prevailing depression because of the opportunities it had given for consolidating children's library work. This work, which was "lyrical librarianship", was based on love, the children's library having become "the love-room of the library".

The speaker then called on her colleagues to recognize children's librarians as experts! In contrast a delegate from Sheffield asked for a less sentimental attitude towards children's libraries, and said that women in libraries should cultivate a more masculine attitude towards their work. Wherever library work with children has been practised, responsible librarians have endeavoured to strike a balance between these two extremes of opinion.

In 1942 L. R. McColvin presented his report to the Library Association on *The Public Library System of Great Britain*. He discovered that standards of service to children varied enormously, and that in 40% of the urban central libraries which he visited there was no separate children's department. Particularly deplorable was the fact that 25% of these libraries were in towns with populations in excess of 50,000.

Many of the municipal children's rooms were adapted for the purpose as at Croydon and Herne Hill in 1920. In the same year, the new children's library at Hove comprised a small reference library and reading room which was well furnished and lit. However, during the years of the depression very little development was undertaken until the late 1930's. A very attractive library for children was provided at Lowestoft. New libraries with separate rooms for children which were opened in 1936 included that at St. Pancras, and in 1937 the children's libraries at Deptford, Nottingham, and Stepney were reorganized.

The county service progressed slowly too. A large body of opinion mistakenly regarded the work as being principally for young people in the immediate years after 1919. This was due to the close association with education, and in rural areas the library centres were mainly housed in schools. Counties which adopted the Public Libraries Act later did not manifest this imbalance of service. A large number of counties adopted the Act in the 1920's, among the earliest being Cheshire, Cumberland, Kent, Middlesex, Pembroke, Warwick, and Worcester. Boxes of books were originally taken to centres by carrier or rail, but in 1924 Kent acquired its first van, and was imitated by others, so that in 1926, nine authorities possessed vans. This service was more expensive than carriers or rail, but was the first attempt to bring the library to the village. However, development was slow in the 1930's, and even in 1938, only a minority of county libraries had their own vans. Young people were able to obtain books for study from the students' sections which were housed at county library headquarters.

The 1920's and 1930's were years of experiment, and some interesting projects took place in various parts of the country. At Ipswich the traditional arrangement of the children's library by the Dewey Decimal Classification was abandoned, and the books rearranged by broad topics. Fiction was also classified by topics.

In addition to books it was customary to provide some periodicals in most children's libraries. Frequently the total would reach 20 or 30 titles. However, one library extended its periodicals policy to include the pictorial *Playbox*, *Rainbow*, and *Tiger Tim's Weekly*. The hope was expressed that children would be led to improve their tastes. There was and is no evidence that reading tastes were or are improved by the provision of comics as the first step to better reading.

Activities designed to encourage children to use the library and to awaken interest in reading became widespread in municipal libraries. Seven hundred children participated in a competition at Oxford in 1928 which was designed to teach them the uses of the catalogue and reference books.

Story hours were popular and many libraries had lecture halls which were licensed for film performances. Large audiences of children attended story hours at Chester and Chesterfield in the early 1930's. At a Croydon branch library a reading circle was formed at which standard books such as *Gulliver's Travels* and *Treasure Island* were read and discussed by groups of children. Elementary elocution lessons were given to story-telling assistants at Croydon. Plays and concerts were often performed by the children.

Some libraries produced magazines among which were *The Magic Casement* at Hendon; *Realms of Gold* at Middlesbrough, which was edited by one of the young readers; and *Treasureland* at Fulham. It was estimated in 1936 that there were approximately 25 such magazines in existence which were produced for children.

Book weeks were also a feature of the work. The National Book Council sponsored a *Boys' and Girls' Book Week* in November 1932 and on other occasions. The January 1933 issue of *Realms of Gold* included a description of the book week pageant and exhibition at Middlesbrough. In 1942 the National Book Council issued a report on children's book weeks entitled *An Experiment with Youth*.

The weakness of work with young people in libraries was the inability to retain the interest of teenagers. During the years after World War I there were slight signs of awareness of this problem on the part of librarians and others interested in the work. A C.U.K.T. system of book grants to youth clubs was initiated in 1926, and Charles Nowell, a leading public librarian, was invited to compile a catalogue from which grew *Books To Read* in 1930. This was supplemented in 1932 and issued as a new work by W. C. Berwick Sayers in 1936 entitled *Books for Youth: a classified and annotated guide for young readers* (Library Association). This was a very detailed work but the bulk of the contents was irrelevant to the needs or abilities of the majority of teenagers. The Kenyon Report (1927) stressed the value of public libraries providing collections for this age group.

Attempts were made to institute intermediate libraries for adolescents, which were sometimes special rooms but were more usually sections of the adult library. An intermediate library was established at Walthamstow in 1924 with a bookstock of 4000 volumes, a total which had increased to 6000 in 1933. A section of the new Northern Branch at Nottingham was devoted to books for teenagers in 1923, and in succeeding years the policy was adopted as other new branches were opened. Provision was also made at the new central library in Nottingham when it was extended in 1932. The concept of a section in the adult library was preferable to a separate department as it gave teenagers the prestige of belonging to the senior department but with access to specially selected material if they wished to use it. At Coventry from 1929 intermediate collections were housed in both adult and children's libraries, but the scheme was abandoned by 1934. There was scarcely any special provision made for adolescents when Eric Leyland's *The Public Library and the Adolescent* was published in 1937. He included a 90 page list of books which he recommended as suitable for teenagers.

The concept of co-operation between schools and public libraries was repeated with continuous approval in reports from Kenyon (1927) and McColvin (1942) on public libraries, to those of the Carnegie and Hadow committees. Co-operation was undertaken between librarians and teachers in the encouragement of children to use the public library for recreation and for homework facilities; the gathering of classes in the public library for instruction in the use of books; the provision of booklists; and the supply of books and other materials to schools, either as permanent collections or as loans to be changed at intervals. Education committees normally financed the schemes, whilst the public libraries provided the service.

Numerous schemes of book supply to schools were operated from 1920, examples of which were at Blackburn, Bromley, Burnley, Cardiff, Coventry, Hendon, Lancaster, Leeds, Liverpool, Margate, Stretford, Westhoughton, and Wiltshire. This policy was administered in reverse at Gateshead and Walthamstow where education committee grants were used to finance children's collections at the public library.

At Leicester, library rooms were established in chosen schools in each of the areas into which the town was divided for educational purposes in and after 1928. These libraries were reserved in the mornings for the school in which they were situated, and in the afternoons, classes received instruction from the librarian. From 5 to 7.30 p.m., however, children from other elementary schools in the area were admitted, and from 8 to 9.30 p.m. facilities were offered to students from evening schools.

On one particular point librarians and teachers were frequently opposed to each other. McColvin in his report recommended that

> . . . unless geographical considerations prevent, children should be served with their general reading in their public libraries and not in the schools.

This attitude was reinforced in the post-war proposals of the Library Association in 1943, and in the Memorandum on *Work with Young People* in 1945, which stated that "the major part of the responsibility" for providing a library service for children "should now rest with the library authorities". These views were not shared by the School Library Association, and many would suggest that the Library Association was arrogantly presumptuous in its analysis of the needs of the situation. This insular attitude was unlikely to further either co-operative ventures or the influence of libraries on children.

CHAPTER 19

Secondary Education For All
1945–1965

BETWEEN 1945 and 1964 the school population rose from 5 to over 7 million, of which 71 % were in primary schools. It had been the original intention to introduce the new school leaving age of 15 in 1945, but this was delayed until 1947. In 1964 the Ministry of Education was superseded by the Department of Education and Science, and the Minister by a Secretary of State, a development which signified recognition of education as a major section of government responsibility.

The situation in secondary education improved considerably. When the publication *Secondary Education For All: a new drive*, was issued in 1958 it was revealed that within a decade the number of children at school aged 15 and over had risen from 187,000 to 290,600 and there were indications that the increase would continue. This progress was not solely confined to grammar schools, where the sixth forms had almost doubled between 1948 and 1958, but was true of modern schools, where the numbers of pupils aged 15+ had increased to 38,000.

In 1959 was published the report of the Crowther Committee, entitled *15 to 18*, which considered the education of young people in that age group. The desirability was emphasized of raising the school leaving age, and recommendations were made regarding courses in modern schools, and the work of sixth forms in grammar schools. The education of pupils of average and less than average ability aged 13 to 16 who were either at school or undergoing further education, was investigated by the Newsom Committee, whose report was published in 1963 entitled *Half Our*

182

Future. In the face of international competition and the advance of technical achievement, not only was it necessary to provide for more skilled workers, but also for a better educated and adaptable labour force to meet the new demands. With this in mind, the Newsom Committee recommended that the school leaving age should be raised, courses related more closely to occupational interests, and a longer school day spent in balanced proportions of curricular and extra-curricular activities.

In 1944 the vision was seen of a secondary school system in which all students were educated according to their needs, but in which no category was superior to another. This ideal had not materialized, and the Newsom Committee was concerned for pupils who discovered that their modern school fell short of their expectations. The provision of an irrelevant education was wasted on young people who were not necessarily aware of possible improvements, but recognized the shortcomings of the existing situation. Many educationists were hopeful that the introduction of comprehensive schools, which increased through government support after 1964, would provide a more realistic form of secondary education for all.

On the subject of further education, a pamphlet entitled *Day Release* was issued in 1964, in which it was shown that the Education Act of 1944 was not being applied. It was recommended that by 1969/70 at least 250,000 extra young people should obtain release from employment, which at the rate of 50,000 per year would result in a doubling of the numbers which then obtained. The passing of an Industrial Training Act in 1964, and the recommendations of *Day Release* were expected to result in major improvement, but in view of the successive legislation which has not been enforced in the past, it would be unwise to predict the outcome in this particular instance.

Through the years the entry of young people into institutions of higher education had increased. When the Barlow Committee on *Scientific Manpower* reported in 1946, rather less than 2% of the population went to universities. Only 20% of young people whose intelligence equated with the better students at university actually had the opportunity of higher education. There was, the Barlow Committee believed, "clearly an ample reserve of intelligence in the country to allow both a doubling of university numbers, and at the same time a raising of standards". The Robbins Report on *Higher Education* (1963) proposed that the percentage of the age group undergoing full-time higher education should be raised from 8% to 17% by 1980, and in common with the Barlow Committee, the investigations of Robbins "suggested the existence of large reservoirs of untapped ability in the population, especially among girls". Many educationists have taken issue with this view, but it does at least sound a note of optimism which gives hope for the future.

Local surveys of reading after the war in such areas as Brighton (1948), Burton-on-Trent (1949/50), Leeds (1953), Swansea (1954), and Kent (1954), suggested that backwardness and illiteracy increased considerably during World War II. A Committee was appointed in 1947 by the Minister of Education to consider the extent of the illiteracy, and in 1948 a reading test was devised by Dr. A. F. Watts and Professor P. E. Vernon. The new and pre-war tests were answered by 800 primary and secondary school children, and the scores compared, but no final solution could be reached as the standards of all the pre-war tests were local and differed one from another. However, averages were compiled, and whilst the proportions of backward readers were larger than pre-war, the number of pupils leaving school almost or completely illiterate was found to be approximately 5% less than was often claimed. Further surveys were conducted in 1952, 1956, 1961 and 1964, and the improvement in standards of reading proved to be progressive.

There were 35 graduated questions in the Watts–Vernon test to be answered in a period of 10 minutes. The proportion of pupils aged 15 which scored 20 or more points rose from 59% in 1948 to 61% in 1952, and 66% in 1956, and this improvement was almost entirely shown in the non-selective schools. The detailed results of these national surveys were contained in the Ministry's pamphlet *Standards of Reading, 1948–1956* (1957), and those related to the local investigations in Dr. Joyce Morris' *Reading in the Primary School* (1959). The Newsom Report (1963) showed the gain in literacy as follows.

Year	Reading test (average score)	Reading age (gain in months)
1948	18·0	—
1956	18·9	6
1961	21·3	23

In 1966 the Department of Education's report on *Progress in Reading* confirmed a continued progress and showed an improvement on the estimated pre-war levels of reading. The standard attained by 50% of the boys and girls aged 11 in 1948 was attained by 75% in 1964. There was a corresponding advance among boys and girls aged 15.

It was impossible to determine which of the contemporary methods of teaching reading was best, and there was evidence to suggest that different methods developed different aspects. The phonic method appeared to improve word recognition, whilst the look and say approach furthered comprehension. Large numbers of primers were published after 1944, but among the most popular were the earlier *Beacon Readers* (1922) and *The Happy Venture Readers* (1939). However, in the mid-1950's there were signs that the *Beacons* were being superseded by series such as *The Janet and John Books* (1951). Backward readers were retained in infants' schools for a longer period than normal to bring them up to standard, but in other cases they were placed in special classes. If children encountered prolonged difficulty in reading it was increasingly believed that the reason was due to an error of judgement in the assessment of reading readiness, or in the selection of a method unsuitable to the individual child. The chronic shortage of teachers left much to be desired, and in truth any progress was made against this, economic difficulties, a high birthrate, and oversized classes.

In 1962 an Augmented Roman Alphabet was introduced by John A. Downing in his book *tω bεε or not to be*, which was revised in 1964 with the title *The Initial Teaching Alphabet*. This alphabet was devised by Sir James Pitman from original designs made by his grandfather, and consisted of 43 characters. Where it has been practised the results have been good and a transfer made to books printed in the traditional alphabet. Percy Lord, the Chief Education Officer for Lancashire, in 1964 stated his belief that I.T.A. was "one of the most promising developments we have had in education for many years", a view which was widely supported among responsible educationists. In 1965 it was claimed that over 700 schools in the United Kingdom were participating in this method of teaching phonics, and in addition to numerous new primers, others were printed in I.T.A. Supplementary books have included the works of A. A. Milne and Beatrix Potter.

Another experiment which was pioneered by Dr. Caleb Gattegno entailed the printing of words in colour so that letters or groups of letters were coloured according to the sound they represented. In this way, written English was rendered phonetic for teaching purposes whilst the conventional spelling was maintained.

The use of books in schools has been encouraged by the work of the School Library Association, which has issued a number of very helpful booklists, including *Eleven to Fifteen: a booklist of non-fiction* (1950, latest edition 1963), *Modern Adult Fiction for School and College Libraries* (1955), *Primary School Library Books* (1960, latest edition 1965), and *French from Five to Fifteen* (1962). Reviews of current material have appeared in *The School Librarian*. The National Book League has produced similarly useful bibliographies such as *The Education Book Guide*, which was issued annually from 1956 to 1964, *Additions to your School Library* (1964), *School Library Books: Non-Fiction* (1965), and a number of smaller lists. Touring exhibitions on various subjects have also been of value.

Books for backward readers assumed an unprecedented importance in the post-war years. Guides to selection included the surveys of books for backward readers compiled by the Bristol University Institute of Education (1956 and 1962), the National Book League's *Help in Reading*, Alan Pullen's *Words of Persuasion* (1962), and the Library Association County Libraries Group's *The Reluctant Reader*. Some local authority library and education departments produced special lists of books for backward readers, and particularly outstanding were the Kent Education Committee, and Lindsey and Holland County Library lists. New books were reviewed in such periodicals as *Forward Trends, The Slow Learning Child*, and *The Use of English*, and lists were readily available from publishers. Particular credit was due to authors who were prepared to write suitable books for backward readers, including John Anderson, Geoffrey Boumphrey, John Duncan, Keith Gardner, and Gertrude Keir; and to their publishers, Harrap, Oxford University Press, and Pitman, the latter of which introduced copies printed in the Initial Teaching Alphabet.

The Ministry of Education encouraged schools to use books in its pamphlets *The School Library* (1952) and *The Use of Books* (1964), and the Inspectors' library known as *The Tann Collection of Books For Use in Primary Schools* has stimulated a great deal of interest since its formation in 1949. For many years a number of colleges of education have attempted to train student teachers in the use of books, but this kind of activity has only been accelerated since 1960.

Additional assistance to teachers has been rendered through model collections, and booklists produced by L.E.A.s, public libraries, and institutes of education. The publishing trade has been quick to recognize the increased demand for information books, and has not only ensured that they are attractive and interesting, but has kept teachers informed of new publications through a vast amount of publicity material. In addition to *The School Librarian*, information relating to new books has been contained in *The School Book Review* (1959), special issues of *The Times Educational Supplement*, and a whole range of professional handbooks and subject journals. References to the vast number of information books which have become available since 1950 have been made in the chapter on "Children's Literature" from 1945 to 1965, because the distinction between books for use in schools and recreative non-fiction has virtually disappeared.

Although so many books were available and so many guides to their selection were published, insufficient money was generally available for their purchase. In practice less than 1% of the national educational expenditure was allocated to the acquisition of books. The Association of Education Committees made recommendations regarding expenditure on stationery and text-books in 1965. Primary schools were assumed to be making adequate provision if they spent 52s. 6d. per head in a year of which 26s. 6d. was allocated to books, whilst similar provision in secondary schools entailed an expenditure of 100s. (45s. for books).

In primary schools education was only regarded as at its best where books were used as an integral part of learning, but large numbers of schools were still not sufficiently committed to these methods of instruction. Children would be incapable of active learning unless they could use books for themselves. A travesty of active learning with books has been observed in the copying of long undigested passages, a sure sign that the children have not been trained to use books correctly. The most suitable use of books both factual and imaginative has been when the need has arisen out of the spontaneous interests of children with or without tutorial stimulation.

The Ministry's *Primary Education* (1959) suggested that in infants' classes:

> . . . children can choose and take down books for themselves, sit quietly turning the pages, absorbed perhaps in the pictures and finding words to talk about them . . . Others may already be turning to books for pictures of things they know and want to know more about . . . Thus from the very beginning, the enjoyment and the use of books form a part of normal life at school.

Having progressed to the junior school it was imperative that a graduated supply of books should be maintained both standard and modern, from an increasingly large selection. Once more the books should not be available for short periods each week but whenever they were required. It was not necessary for the books to have been especially written for children, and therefore, difficult books were quite suitable, particularly if the curiosity of children had been aroused. *Primary Education* included references to such works as the *Iliad*, the *Odyssey*, the Norse sagas, Bede's *Ecclesiastical History of England*, Froissart's *Chronicles*, Joinville and Villehardouin's *Memoirs of the Crusades*, Hakluyt's *Voyages*, and Pepys' *Diary*, most of which were available in Dent's *Everyman Library* at prices ranging from 8*s*. to 12*s*. 6*d*. per volume. Naturally, many passages in these books would be quite unsuitable for children, but any difficulties could be removed by teachers. In geography, many teachers were still committed to the use of textbooks, but an increasing number were providing books in greater quantities, together with such reference material as encyclopaedias and gazetteers. The expansion of the curriculum in primary schools in the 1960's resulted in the acquisition of books in French, as well as material on the more traditional subjects.

The pattern of active learning was broken at the secondary stage, particularly in grammar schools, in which the General Certificate of Education was a preoccupation, and to a lesser extent, in modern schools, where the possibility of such a situation could increase after the introduction of the Certificate of Secondary Education in 1965. However, the Newsom Committee recommended the appointment of general subjects teachers in modern schools, which would, if implemented, result in a more flexible curriculum, and with it, a wider use of books.

Many children left junior schools without having mastered the techniques of reading, and would certainly require help in the secondary schools. The association of reading with years of failure need not necessitate a permanent aversion to the practice, and in this context the Newsom Committee commented that

> ... even at 14 it is not too late to make a fresh start, provided that the start is really fresh; it is useless to go on boring the pupils of this age with books from the primary school.

The problem here, however, was that there was an inadequate selection of books for teenagers, with less than average reading ability, and under these circumstances, the view of the Newsom Committee was a pious ideal.

An interest in practical subjects, as in the modern school, had in the past resulted in a neglect of books. However, it was necessary that teenagers should be acquainted with the ideas of craftsmen to stimulate their own creativity, and for this reason well-illustrated books dealing with the history of such subjects as costume, architecture, and painting, were of value. Reading in this manner could lead young people in turn to art galleries, museums and theatres. The truth is that every effort to interest these pupils in reading must be made, and progressive educationists believed that a commencement towards a literary goal could only succeed if the actual interests of the young people were considered.

In science, background studies could well be read by the more able pupils, especially in grammar schools, where the preoccupation with textbooks was most to be observed. Examples of this type of literature could include Konrad Lorenz' *King Solomon's Ring* (1961), Gavin Maxwell's *Ring of Bright Water* (1962), Rachel Carson's *Silent Spring* (1963), Isaac Asimov's *Inside the Atom* (1956), Ritchie Calder's *Science Makes Sense* (1955) or the Penguin Science Surveys.

Encouragement in reading was hindered by major obstacles. The Newsom Committee pointed out that many adults passed their time "quite happily with little reading", a fact of which young people were aware. On the other hand, they knew that they would not be at ease in the complex modern world if they could not read, and a way must be found by teachers to strike a reasonable balance. It may be due to the heightened interest, not only in the techniques, but also in the continuance of reading, that the level of literacy was seen to rise in the years after 1948.

However, as was demonstrated in the chapters which included references to literacy in the 19th century, the definition of the word was not constant. In the last decade, the Newsom and Crowther Reports have added their weight to this contention. They have emphasized that the possession of literacy must be closely related to the abilities of the individual, and the demands made on him by society if he is to take his place in the community:

> Literacy, is not a single skill, something achieved once for all with the power to translate written symbols into sounds. It involves the power to invest words with meaning, to recognize the ideas which somebody else wishes them to convey and to use them oneself to express the thoughts which without their help would remain fleeting and inchoate [Newsom Report].

The Watts–Vernon Test did not simply measure the ability to read but also required a wide and precise personal vocabulary. A proven literacy at a particular time is something which will not remain constant, but continue to rise throughout life to meet new situations as they arise.

Crowther developed this theme (although in practice it antedated Newsom by 5 years) to imply that if a scientist could not communicate effectively with those who had undergone a literary education, then he was illiterate. This Committee coined the word "numeracy", which it defined as "the mirror image of literacy", and which was as necessary to the well-educated arts scholar as literacy to the scientist. The difficulty of achieving such an ideal state which would serve to integrate the two cultures, was partly due to the pressure of specialist subjects, but the Crowther Committee claimed that the minority time could be organized to ensure a "balanced education". Sixth formers, at the end of their courses in grammar schools, should be "on the way to becoming" well read men, both "numerate as well as literate".

The literacy of the individual will determine his contribution to society in a meritocracy, and no effort should be spared in ensuring the availability of suitable material which can be related in adequate quantities, to his ability. A deficiency of books suitable for particular age groups or ranges of intelligence, must be a matter for concern to all who are dedicated to the furtherance of education, either as a means to individual development, or as a national investment.

CHAPTER 20

A Second Golden Age in Children's Literature 1945-1965

THERE was a shortage of paper after the war, and supplies were allocated to printers on a quota system. The annual publication of children's books did not exceed 1000 volumes until 1947, but the increase was rapid in the 1950's and 1960's so that in 1965 the total was approximately 2500. A substantial quantity of good quality literature was published, reaching a peak in the 1950's, but not maintaining the same level in the 1960's. However, even in the latter decade, the quality was higher than in the years prior to 1950.

An interest in children's literature was demonstrated in the publication of a number of histories and criticisms in Britain, which included Roger Lancelyn Green's *Tellers of Tales* (Ward, 1946), Janet Adam Smith's *Children's Illustrated Books* (Collins, 1948), Geoffrey Trease's *Tales Out of School* (Heinemann, 1948), Frank Eyre's *Twentieth Century Children's Books* (Longmans, 1952), Percy Muir's *English Children's Books*, 1600 *to* 1900 (Batsford, 1954), Margery Fisher's *Intent upon Reading* (Brock-hampton, 1961), Marcus Crouch's *Treasure Seekers and Borrowers* (Library Association, 1962), M. F. Thwaite's *From Primer to Pleasure* (Library Association, 1963), and John Rowe Townsend's *Written for Children* (Garnet Miller, 1965). Later editions were published of Green, Trease, and Fisher. In addition, the Library Association instituted the Kate Greenaway Medal in 1955, which was usually awarded annually to an outstanding example of children's book illustration.

The advent of television after 1945 exercised an influence over the reading of children. Initially the presence of television in a home tended to result in a reduction in reading, but after a time it frequently prompted children to read for a number of reasons. Numerous young children received their first introduction to books through this medium, whilst older children were able to develop in books interests which had been aroused and to read stories which had been dramatized. There were enormous possibilities for co-operation between the British Broadcasting Corporation and the Independent Television Authority, on the one hand, and teachers and librarians on the other. If advance notice was given to librarians of books planned for dramatization during a particular period, they could then ensure that a supply was available to meet the anticipated demand.

Two organizations were formed during the early 1960's which were capable of a potential influence on books for children. The Children's Book Circle (1962) consisted of children's book editors, and all the leading publishers were represented; and the Children's Writers' Group (1963) was formed within the Society of Authors to improve the standards of writing for children. In contrast with earlier periods the emphasis in children's books was transferred from various types of fantasy to the factual information books which could be used with equal success both in school work and for recreational purposes.

Reality was brought into fiction in the emergence of family/ adventure stories with lower-, middle- and working-class backgrounds in the tradition of Eve Garnett. Authors in this category included Eric Allen, Anne Barrett, E. W. Hildick, Elizabeth Stucley, John Rowe Townsend, and Geoffrey Trease. None of these writers was outstanding since each deliberately restricted their scope, but all were readable. The most prominent exponent of the family/adventure story was William Mayne, whilst other writers were Lucy Boston, Philippa Pearce, Sheena Porter, Philip Turner, and Elfrida Vipont.

Well written adventure stories, mainly at sea, were produced by Richard Armstrong; and science fiction and space adventures were well represented by David Craigie, Donald Suddaby and Hugh Walters. The latter group of fiction was not particularly popular with young people in the 1950's, but was received more favourably in the 1960's.

After the War school stories did not maintain their position, but were revived in and after 1955 by William Mayne, whose books were set in a cathedral choir school. Girls continued to read school stories, principally by authors of a previous generation, but the books were concerned more with personal relationships than with education in its academic sense.

The greatest post-war impact in fiction was made by the historical novel which exhibited a high degree of literary art and historical accuracy. Authors who made a major contribution in this field included Hester Burton, J. G. Fyson, Cynthia Harnett, Barbara Leonie Picard, Rosemary Sutcliff (Fig. 24), Geoffrey Trease, Henry Treece, and Ronald Welch. Historical fiction gives scope for imaginative writing which is either impossible or very difficult to accomplish in family stories.

Along with historical fiction, fantasy also maintained high standards. Credit was due to the Oxford University Press in the 1940's and 1950's for reissuing work by Walter de la Mare and Eleanor Farjeon, so that a new generation of children could enjoy their magic. Leading writers of fantasy during the period were Alan Garner, C. S. Lewis, and Mary Norton, who created respectively, the horrific world of Elidor, the allegorical Narnia, and the haunts of the Borrowers.

Numerous editions of the tales of Andersen, Grimm and Perrault, and the *Fables* of Aesop and *Tales from the Arabian Nights* were available, some of them beautifully produced. Outstanding work was undertaken by Roger Lancelyn Green, Barbara Leonie Picard, Ian Serraillier, Rosemary Sutcliff, and others, in retelling the myths of Greece, Rome, and the North; the legends of Roland, Arthur, and Robin Hood. The literary and folk traditions of the world were readily available to British children as never before.

Animal fantasy was represented by Margery Sharp's mice. Phenomenal success was enjoyed among younger children in the late 1950's and 1960's by the books of Michael Bond, the creator of

FIG. 24.   Title page from Rosemary Sutcliff's *Knight's Fee*. 1960.
(By courtesy of Oxford University Press.)

Paddington the bear. Pony stories maintained some popularity and were written by Monica Edwards, and Christine and Diana Pullein-Thompson. There was a dearth of British authors who wrote wild animal stories in the tradition of Ballantyne and Kipling, and the deficiency was met to some extent by importations from the Commonwealth, Europe, and the United States. It is true that books were available by Gerald Durrell and Henry Williamson, but they were not especially written for children.

Poetry books achieved unparalleled peaks in the compositions of John Betjeman, Robert Graves, Ted Hughes, James Reeves, and Ian Serraillier, and allusion has been made to the reissue of work by Walter de la Mare and Eleanor Farjeon. Outstanding anthologies were compiled by Edward Blishen, Roger Lancelyn Green, Geoffrey Grigson, and Janet Adam Smith, whilst collections of nursery rhymes were edited by Barbara Ireson, Kathleen Lines and Iona and Peter Opie. In addition, a number of well-balanced prose anthologies were compiled by Hester Burton, Eileen Colwell, David Holbrook, and Kathleen Lines. The practice of reading aloud to children in schools encouraged the production of anthologies for different age groups.

Picture books maintained the high standards set by Ardizzone, Brooke, Caldecott, and Beatrix Potter in the 1960's but in the previous decade the Greenaway Medal was not awarded on two occasions. Perhaps a British contribution was stimulated through the appearance of many delightful American picture books imported by Woodfield and Stanley from the United States, such as Helen Sewell's *Blue Barns* and Dorothy Lathrop's *Animals of the Bible*. Whatever the reason, a high standard of draughtsmanship and colour appreciation was displayed in the picture books of Victor Ambrus, John Burningham, Antony Maitland, Gerald Rose, William Stobbs, and Brian Wildsmith. Many books were printed on the continent by craftsmen in Austria, Czechoslovakia, Germany, Italy (the finest work) and Switzerland, and were made available in excellent editions at more reasonable prices than were usually possible in Britain. The experiment with continental printing was initiated by Paul Hamlyn.

Although the Greenaway Medal was for outstanding book illustration it was mainly awarded, with few exceptions, to picture books, one of which was C. Walter Hodges' *Shakespeare's Theatre* (1964). However, the quality of book illustration was not reflected in the absence of attention given to it by the Library Association. Outstanding work was performed by such artists as Victor Ambrus, Susan Einzig, Charles Keeping, Joan Kiddell-Monroe, William Papas, Alice and Martin Provensen, William Stobbs, and many others.

It would be impossible to do justice to the wide range of non-fiction which was published. This development was made necessary by the greatly increased demand for books of this kind by school and public libraries, and by the general public. Many publishers issued series on broad subjects of geography, history, and science, which were very similar to each other. The amount of duplication was perhaps unnecessary and was not only confined to broad subjects but also extended to more specific topics such as biology, ancient history, and modern Europe.

Many of the series were not of a high standard either of content or production, and indexes, where they were provided were often inadequate. It must be admitted that the situation in this latter respect frequently improved in books for older children. Very few non-fiction books were awarded the Carnegie Medal, successful examples being Agnes Allen's *The Story of Your Home* (1949), Edward Osmond's *A Valley Grows Up* (1953), and I. W. Cornwall's *The Making of Man* (1960). Younger children in the period were fortunate to have access to the useful and usually attractive *Ladybird Books* which were published by Wills & Hepworth, and which were not only available in the traditional alphabet but also in the Initial Teaching Alphabet.

In contrast to being a neglected category of children's books, non-fiction became prolific, but quality was not always maintained as publishers stampeded to profit in a market which guaranteed financial success. They have a basic interest in financial returns and for this reason are not well placed to contribute satisfactorily to the growth of literacy.

Many outstanding quick reference books were produced, prominent among which were *Oxford Junior Encyclopaedia* in 13 volumes (1948/56, new edition 1964), and Children's Britannica in 12 volumes (1960); *Cassell's Picture Dictionary* (1952), *Thorndike Junior Dictionary* (1955), *Oxford School Dictionary* (1960), and *The Hamish Hamilton Children's Dictionary* (1963); and a wide range of atlases. There were very few reference books of other kinds for children, and use was made of standard works which were available in libraries.

Authors from the United States continued to exercise an influence on British children. Family stories were made available by Joseph Krumgold, Lois Lenski, Ruth Sawyer, and Laura Ingalls Wilder; historical stories by Harold Keith and Elizabeth G. Speare; geographical and animal stories by Meindert Dejong and Nicholas Kalashnikoff. There was an influx of non-fiction published by D. C. Heath, Holt–Rinehart, and others, from which the distinction between textbooks and information books had been removed. These books were usually attractively produced with clear type and useful rather than ornamental illustrations in superb colours.

The numbers of translations of children's books in Britain after World War II rose enormously, to emphasize the greater degree of communication between different countries. At no time before 1950 did the number of translations published in one year exceed 18, but in 1960 they totalled 63; in 1961, 91, a record number; and never less than 59. It appeared to many in the mid-1960's that a slight decline having commenced in the standard of British children's books, the best was being maintained in the publication of works from other countries.

The majority of outstanding translations were family and adventure stories, and authors included, from France, Paul Berna; from Austria, Karl Bruckner; from Holland, Rutgers Van der Loeff; from Sweden, Harry Kullman and Astrid Lindgren; and from South Africa, P. H. Nortje. Historical novels were written by the eminent Hans Baumann of Germany, and stories of wild animals by the prolific and versatile René Guillot of France.

Important fiction from Commonwealth countries, particularly from Australia, was published in Britain. Contributors from Australia included H. F. Brinsmead, Nan Chauncy, Mary Elwyn Patchett, Ivan Southall, and Eleanor Spence.

The availability of well-written books, however, did not mean that they were read by the majority of British children. A survey by the staff and students of the Westfield Training College in Birmingham in 1950 into the reading habits of *Eighty Thousand Adolescents* revealed that approximately 25% of the boys and 20% of the girls had not read a book within a period of 6 months. The comment was made that "many of the 15 to 18 year old members of our society are little more than barely literate . . . ".

The Smith–Harrap survey of *Boys' and Girls' Reading Habits* (1957) showed that the most popular author with all boys was Captain W. E. Johns. The girls' equivalent was Enid Blyton. Also popular with boys were Arthur Ransome, Richmal Crompton and Percy Westerman; while girls favoured L. M. Alcott, Angela Brazil, Arthur Ransome and Noel Streatfeild. This represents a greater interest in more recent authors than was shown in the Jenkinson survey of 1940, but there is a complete absence of authors who began to write after 1945.

Young people also stated their interest in writers of adult novels such as Charles Dickens, Sir Arthur Conan Doyle, Agatha Christie, C. S. Forester, H. Rider Haggard and Nevil Shute. In the general list of preferences, of 22 authors listed, only 10 wrote especially for children and of these only Ransome and Streatfeild were recognized as authors of merit. The principal reason why most of the interest was in adult writers, was because there were so few authors who wrote for the teenage group. The Library Association *Books for Young People* volume which catered for adolescents listed only approximately 25 authors who wrote specifically for teenagers out of a total of 140. The works of a number of adult authors who wrote in the 1950's were read by teenagers, including books by Richard Church, Ian Fleming, C. S. Forester, William Golding, Hammond Innes, Iris Murdoch, and C. P. Snow. Various experts in the 1960's discerned a trend in teenagers reading books for adults at an earlier age than previously.

The number of authors who wrote for teenagers increased slowly. The main British contribution was from historical novelists such as Hester Burton, Barbara Leonie Picard and Rosemary Sutcliff. It was almost as if writers were inhibited by teenage problems, and could only discuss them if the impact was broken by a time barrier. Historical novels from other countries for teenagers were by Hans Baumann, Harold Keith, and Elizabeth G. Speare. However, contemporary life was reviewed by Richard Armstrong in his career–adventure stories, and by William Mayne, Elfrida Vipont, and Barbara Willard in many of their family stories. A major contribution was made by Australian novels in the writings of M. E. Patchett, H. F. Brinsmead, and others, who were beginning to appear in the mid-1960's. However, such books were for the minority of teenagers.

Book prices rose startlingly in the post-war years, as will be demonstrated by the following table. The sum in the first column is the initial price; the other two columns list the price of the same book in 1955 and 1965:

		1955	1965
1950 Lewis: *The Lion, the Witch and the Wardrobe*	8s. 6d.	9s. 6d.	12s. 6d.
1951 Harnett: *The Wool Pack*	11s. 6d.	11s. 6d.	16s.
1952 Norton: *The Borrowers*	9s. 6d.	9s. 6d.	13s. 6d.

Between 1950 and 1955 the prices of most children's books ranged from 8s. 6d., but between 1956 and 1960 they rose to 12s. 6d. In the 1960's prices rose steeply from 1963; for example, William Mayne's *Sand* (1964) cost 18s., Rosemary Sutcliff's *The Mark of the Horse Lord* (1965) cost 17s. 6d., and Philip Turner's *Grange at High Force* (1965) cost 16s. Picture book prices also rose steeply. Ardizzone's *Tim All Alone* (1956) cost 10s. 6d., Rose's *Old Winkle and the Seagulls* (1960), 12s. 6d., but Ambrus' *Three Poor Tailors* (1965) 16s.

Earlier books increased greatly in price. For example, A. A. Milne's *Winnie the Pooh* (7s. 6d. in 1926) was 10s. 6d. in 1965, and Tolkien's *The Hobbit* (7s. 6d. in 1937) was 13s. 6d. Leslie Brooke's *The Golden Goose Book*, which cost 5s. in 1905, was 12s. 6d. in 1955, and 20s. in 1965; and Wanda Gág's *Millions of Cats* was 2s. 6d. in 1929, 4s. 6d. in 1955, and 8s. 6d. in 1965. Editions of Dent's *Illustrated Children's Classics* showed similar tendencies. The Dent edition of Mrs. Molesworth's *Cuckoo Clock* was 9s. 6d. in 1955 and 16s. in 1965, and *Robinson Crusoe* rose from 9s. 6d. to 13s. 6d.

It should be remembered that in these years society was reasonably affluent, and might have been expected to have purchased more books. Price rises of this magnitude which were made necessary by rises in the costs of labour and materials, were not conducive to book purchase by a people, the majority of whom were not convinced of either the value of reading or the building of a personal collection.

However, in a parallel development to the price spiral was that of the paperback. Although in 1965 standard children's fiction might be expected to cost as much as 20s., large numbers of works of varying literary standards became available in paper covers, and could cost as little as 3s. 6d. The *Puffin* series had grown rapidly since its inception in the 1940's and had been supplemented by the *Peacock* series for teenagers in the 1960's. More popular authors such as Enid Blyton, Richmal Crompton, and W. E. Johns, became available in the paper covered *Armada* books, and various of the older publishing firms began to contribute to the paperback market.

Opportunities were therefore offered as never before for young people to purchase books which they could assemble into personal collections. Small bookshops were opened in many schools and book clubs were inaugurated in order to encourage reading. It will be shown in the next chapter that improved standards in public libraries ensured reading facilities for all children who were prepared to take advantage of the services provided.

Large numbers of young people continued to read comics of

various descriptions. Many of the earlier papers ceased to exist, such as *Chatterbox* in 1948, *Mickey Mouse* in 1955, *The Girl's Own Paper* (which had become *Heiress* in 1950) in 1956, and *The Children's Newspaper* in 1965. However, new periodicals were introduced such as *Collins' Magazine for Boys and Girls* in 1948, which was at first printed in Canada due to the paper shortage, but when the controls were removed in 1950, the magazine was produced in Britain.

In 1950 the Hulton Press issued *Eagle* which was well-produced in brilliant colours, clear type, and good quality paper. The circulation of this paper rose to 1 million copies per week. Hulton's published *Girl* in 1951 in order to cater for both sexes. In 1952, Thomson's *Lion* appeared for older boys, and was representative of a new type of British comic for older children after 1950. For young children, Hulton's *Robin* appeared in 1953 and *Swift* in 1954.

However, in the following decade, the sales of these papers decreased until in 1964 their consumption had dropped by 50%, although this was from 16 to 8 million copies each week. There was competition between the publishers for the potential readership, and new publications were issued such as Thomson's *Hornet* in 1963, and *Wham* in 1964. Veterans from the 1930's continued to survive such as *Dandy*, *Beano*, and *Hotspur*, whilst *Rover* and *Wizard* were combined. None of these publications cost more than 6*d.* and some were as little as 3*d.* each, prices which may be compared with the ill-fated *The Children's Newspaper*, which cost 9*d.* in 1965. It was impossible to ascertain whether comics had lost appeal because young people were more sophisticated, or because television was satisfying the demand for visual presentation.

The 1960's witnessed the rise of information periodicals for young people, some of which were reference books in serial form. These included Purnell's *Knowledge* (1961) and Sampson Low's *Understanding Science* (1962). Other periodicals issued weekly were *Look and Learn* (1962) and *Discovering Art* (1964). These maintained a high standard of production and content, and were available at prices which ranged from 2*s*. to 3*s*. 6*d*.

It remains to discuss the descendants of the penny dreadful and the more innocuous sagas of contemporary life. The former were represented by American horror comics which were first imported and then printed from stereotypes in Britain, even though their sale was forbidden in France. Questions were frequently asked in the British Parliament until in 1954 the Children's and Young Persons (Harmful Publications) Act banned the comics, but the embargo was only partially effective. Typical titles of the macabre and sadistic outpourings of twisted minds were *Tales from the Crypt*, *Eerie* and *Ghost Gallery*.

Serial fiction of an equally escapist but more romantic kind was issued in the early 1960's by the Daily Mirror Group (the biggest publishers) which included *Marty*, *Mirabelle* and *Roxy*, all of which enjoyed circulations of at least 200,000 per issue. D. C. Thomson, the pioneer firm, issued *Romeo* and *Bunty*, the latter claiming a circulation of 500,000. A survey of the "love" comics revealed that fewer than 50% of the readers were un-married teenagers, whilst a high proportion were middle-aged women, and another survey of *Teenage Consumer Spending*, conducted by Mark Abrams in 1959, queried the teenagers' psychological need for reading of this character. There could be no doubt surely that a poor domestic background, boredom, a broken home, or other factors necessitated escape to a world where men were charming, and the career of a model or pop singer could be assumed without academic expertise.

The Mark Abrams survey revealed that teenagers spent 3·1% of their £830 million expenditure on books and periodicals, and that 44% of newspaper reading was concentrated on *The Daily Mirror* and *The Daily Sketch*. Smith–Harrap found that the favourite periodicals of boys were *Eagle*, *Reader's Digest*, *The Boy's Own Paper*, and *John Bull*, whilst girls read *Woman*, *Girl* and *Woman's Own*.

It is apparent that literature which varied greatly in quality was available to young people of all ages and intelligences after

1945, at prices which they could afford if they wished to do so. More expensive material was obtainable from the public library. If the general level of literacy were to rise, then at every point there was reading matter available to strengthen its hold on the life of the nation.

CHAPTER 21

Libraries For Children
1945–1965

IN 1950 the School Library Association issued its *School Libraries Today* pamphlet in which it advocated the provision of libraries in both primary and secondary schools, with simple classroom libraries and book corners for the youngest children. During the post-war years the need for libraries in secondary schools was stated in the Ministry of Education's *Building Regulations* (1945), and the Ministry also made grants to the S.L.A. in 1948 and 1949.

Emphasis was given to school libraries by publications of the Ministry of Education, including *The New Secondary Education* (1947), *School and Life* (1947), *The School Library* (1952), *The Story of Post-War School Building* (1957), *Half Our Future* (1963) and *The Use of Books* (1964). An important *Report on School Libraries* was issued by the Education Officer's Department of the London County Council in 1947. The S.L.A. produced *Suggestions For School Libraries* (1953), *The Library in the Primary School* (1958), and various special leaflets on the administration and function of school libraries such as *School Libraries in Library Classrooms* and *Building a Secondary Modern School Library*.

In addition, a large number of useful publications through the years included C. A. Stott's *School Libraries* (Cambridge U.P., 1948), R. G. Ralph's *The Library in Education* (Turnstile Press, 1949), E. Grimshaw's *The Teacher Librarian* (Arnold, 1952), Eric Leyland's *Libraries in Schools* (Oldbourne, 1961), and Ernest Roe's *Teachers, Librarians and Children* (Crosby Lockwood, 1965). Both Stott and Ralph were published in new editions between their publication and 1965.

If libraries were to be truly integrated with the work of schools, it was imperative that the librarian should co-operate closely with his colleagues regarding the selection of material and the planning of library-centred activities. In 1954 the National Book League recommended that bookstock should be considered as essential equipment to be provided within 3 years of a school's opening, and that the annual grant to secondary school libraries should cover increases in stock, replacements, repairs, and subscriptions to periodicals. The L.C.C. report (1947) suggested that in new libraries a basic collection of reference works, essential books on all subjects of the curriculum, and material for recreational reading should be provided. It was considered that an adequate collection would ultimately contain 4 or 5 books for each pupil in junior schools and 8 or 10 in secondary schools, with the addition of loans from the public library or a central educational materials centre.

The Ministry's *The School Library* (1952) was clear that textbooks were not to be included in the library which must contain "individual rather than class" literature. Many schools placed books in all parts of the school where children gathered, whilst others were unfortunately still obsessed with textbook techniques. In many of the schools, the library was accessible all the time, but in others its use was not encouraged.

In the junior schools of Kent in 1954 the average size of collections ranged from 150 to 450 centrally housed volumes, and in conformity to a national pattern, the books were mainly the property of the schools. A capitation allowance varied from 17s. to 28s. depending on the type of organization, the numbers on the roll, and the ages of the pupils. Head teachers could also use for their libraries part of their "amenities" allowance of 2s. 3d. per pupil. It was not uncommon for contributions to be made by parent–teacher associations which had developed after 1944, and frequently school leavers made presentations. Reference books were often expensive but could be obtained through the county library.

School Libraries Today recommended that a teacher should be placed in charge of the library, and should be given at least 3 hours per week for administrative purposes, but the National Book League pressed for the appointment of a qualified librarian. The L.C.C. standards included the appointment of a full-time teacher librarian in schools of 400+ pupils on the grounds that "until such appointments are made the full possibilities of the school library cannot be realized".

In 1947 the Ministry recommenced its short courses for teachers in the use and management of school libraries at Westfield College, London, and after 1949, the experiment was undertaken of a 3 months' course at Homerton College, Cambridge, for qualified teachers. Courses were organized at many teacher training colleges, and in 1958 was commenced the Certificate for Teacher Librarians, which was sponsored by the School Library Association and the Library Association for teachers with 3 years' experience.

The consensus of opinion in primary schools was favourable still to classroom collections. These were particularly helpful to slow learners, who may be induced to progress in familiar surroundings. However, a central library was sometimes successful and increased in value in the junior school. If books were arranged and organized in an orthodox fashion this automatically presented an introduction to practice in the public library.

In its evidence to the Plowden Committee in 1965 the S.L.A. extended the plea for classroom collections for the use of younger children who had recently been transferred to secondary schools, but the general attitude favoured the development of libraries as recommended in the Carnegie Report of 1936. The Newsom Committee considered that "The library ought to be the power house of words and ideas", and that it was as "essential for work in the humanities (though not only in them) as the laboratory is in science". However, the reality was remote from the ideal in spite of the eulogies which had been emitted by official and non-official bodies through the years. In 1963, 60% of the modern schools surveyed on behalf of the Newsom Committee were deficient in library accommodation, and 21% did not include a library room of any kind. Schools with libraries reserved solely for library use consisted of only 26% of the total, whilst in others, the facilities were subject to closure for the purposes of class teaching or restricted through inadequate space.

References were made to the functions of libraries in further education in the Ministry of Education's *Youth's Opportunity* (1946) and *Further Education* (1947). The former dealt with the requirements of the proposed but unrealized county colleges, and recommended "a generous and catholic supply of books" which must be "properly housed". The latter pamphlet advocated the appointment of a trained librarian if the library was to be "an effective educational unit". Libraries in colleges where the young people are in attendance only for one day per week cannot be considered as functioning in the same way as libraries where the student population is present on a full-time or sandwich basis. The integration of the library with the work of the college in these circumstances of day continuation courses is a problem which has not been satisfactorily solved, although some outstanding work has been carried out during the 1960's at the West Ham College of Further Education among other institutions. Standards for colleges of further education were contained in documents issued by the Library Association entitled *College Libraries* (1965) and the Association of Teachers in Technical Institutions entitled *Use of Libraries* (1966).

In the field of public libraries the most hopeful event was the passing of the Public Libraries and Museums Act of 1964. This placed public libraries in England and Wales under the super-vision of the Secretary of State for Education, who with the assistance of Advisory Councils was to ensure that local authori-ties discharged their functions efficiently in "encouraging both adults and children to make full use of the library service". Until this time the adoption of the Public Libraries Act was permissive but it now became compulsory. It became possible for library committees to be appointed in counties, and co-operation was to make provision for the borrowing of books and non-book materials "to meet the general requirements and any special requirements both of adults and children". The references to children were particularly interesting as they showed recognition of a part of library work which had been neglected or ignored in many parts of the country.

The Act was preceded by the report of a committee on *The Structure of the Public Library Service in England and Wales* under the chairmanship of Sir Sidney Roberts in 1959. The Roberts Report estimated that public libraries were used by 33% of the population. In the case of young people, however, the percentage was higher, as was demonstrated in a *Survey of Boys' and Girls' Reading Habits* published in 1957 by the firms of W. H. Smith and George G. Harrap:

	Boys (%)	Girls (%)
Grammar	73·16	82·16
Modern	57·8	70·8

The findings were based on replies from 8000 boys and girls between the ages of 11 and 18 at schools in England and Wales, and the evidence was that not only did girls read more than boys, but that modern school girls read almost as much as grammar school boys.

In 1947 the Library Association began to take a closer interest in work with young people when a special Section was formed. This body was renamed the Youth Libraries Group in 1962, and has undertaken a wide variety of activities including the compilation of surveys, the publication of bibliographies, and the organization of weekend schools and other meetings.

The Youth Libraries Section *Survey* of 1954 revealed a depressing situation as regards public library facilities for children. Some libraries contained one children's book for each child in the area, whilst in others the ratio was one book for 50 children. A majority of libraries stocked reference books but not periodicals. More than 25% of the libraries which were investigated (255 out of 468) did not provide a separate children's room. This survey was revised in 1958/9 and it was still true "that with few exceptions, library authorities were not providing adequate services".

In the post-war years there was very little progress in the building of public libraries owing to the considerable difficulty in obtaining materials and planning permission. Development was accelerated after 1960 and included imaginative provision for young people in both county libraries, such as the West Riding and Kent, and in boroughs such as Eastbourne, Hampstead, Holborn, Hornsey, Luton and Sunderland. At Dover in 1963 a separate central children's library was opened which contrasted with the large numbers of borough and county branch libraries in which no physical divisions were erected between the adult and children's libraries. Examples of the "open plan" branch libraries were to be found at Battersea, Bromley, Cheltenham, Edmonton and Liverpool. Almost without exception central and branch libraries in boroughs, and branches in counties contained facilities for extension activities, encouraging evidence of the increased interest of librarians in this work.

In 1962 the report was published of a Working Party appointed by the Minister of Education on *Standards of Public Library Service in England and Wales*, and on the subject of books for children the point was made that quality was more important than quantity. It was considered that a library providing a basic service should purchase approximately 33% of the children's books published annually in Britain, which in 1960 totalled approximately 2300; in 1962, 2100; and in 1964, 2450. In addition the quantity of duplicates and replacements to be acquired would be an equal number. Therefore a reasonable acquisition of additions and replacements in 1964 was 1630 volumes.

Various bibliographies and booklists were available in the post-war period. The leading guide to children's books was the three-volume Library Association publication *Books For Young People*, which was issued between 1952, with the first edition of Group I; and 1960, with the third edition of Group II. Kathleen Lines produced an outstanding work for the National Book League in 1950 entitled *Four to Fourteen: a library of books for children* (Cambridge U.P.), and a second edition was issued in 1956 which contained approximately 1000 classified entries. The National

Book League's *British Children's Books* was issued in 1963, followed by a new edition in 1964. The selection of new books was assisted by the consultation of the weekly *British National Bibliography* (1950), the weekly *The Bookseller* and its voluminous spring and autumn issues, *The Junior Bookshelf* (1937), Mrs. Margery Fisher's authoritative *Growing Point* (1962), and the responsible *Children's Book News* (1964). An annual publication entitled *The Best Children's Books*, published by Hamish Hamilton and well edited by Naomi Lewis was issued from 1964. In addition, librarians could scrutinize large numbers of colourful publishers' catalogues and prospectuses.

In the Youth Libraries Section *Survey* of 1954, it was revealed that less than 50% of the libraries had appointed a special children's librarian, but this had increased to 62% in 1962. The Roberts Committee expressed the view that there should be "more specialist posts in libraries and more staff qualified to fill them . . . particularly . . . children's librarians". An optional paper on library work with young people was included in the Library Association Final Examination in 1946, but this was removed in 1950 for a few years. For some years after 1954 the Youth Libraries Section Committee and the School of Librarianship at the North West Polytechnic in London co-operated to provide a course of some weeks' duration, but the need for this ceased on the institution of a new syllabus of professional examinations in 1964. Two papers were included, one on Library Service for Young People and another on the Bibliography of Children's Literature. An additional syllabus for post-graduate entrants to the profession was commenced in 1965, in which there were two similar papers relating to work with young people.

The Library Association published a memorandum on the *Duties, Responsibilities, Status and Training of Librarians who Work With Children and Young People* in 1963. Children's librarians were expected to be Associates of the Library Association, and their qualifications and experience were to be reflected in their salary and status as senior officials.

The staffing memorandum stated that "the provision of an

adequate and well-chosen bookstock is but the beginning of the children's librarian's work". Both the *Survey* of 1954 and the Report of the Working Party in 1962 expressed approval at the amount of extension activities undertaken in public libraries, which included displays, story hours, magazines, book weeks, film shows, play-reading groups, quizzes, special clubs, and reading circles. The Working Party commented that most large municipal, some small municipal, and larger county branches, were engaged in this wide range of activities, particularly where qualified librarians had been appointed.

An outstanding *Children's Library Magazine* was produced three times in each year by the Preston Public Library from 1950. Book weeks were held at many libraries including Bootle, Dudley, Luton, Nottingham, Preston, Shrewsbury, and a particularly ambitious programme was undertaken at Lambeth for a number of years. Booklists too, were compiled on a large scale and notable work was produced by county libraries such as Hertford, Kent, Stafford, the West Riding, and Wiltshire: and by the boroughs of Bethnal Green, Chester, Islington and Scunthorpe.

Increasingly, work was undertaken with teenagers, and sections were devoted to this in the Albemarle Report on *The Youth Service in England and Wales* (1960), and that of the Working Party (1962). The acknowledged drift of teenagers from libraries could be countered by the placing of collections in youth clubs with library staff exercising supervision in the capacity of assistant youth leaders. It was not considered that these collections were a substitute for the public library, but they could possibly stimulate reading interests. Some libraries arranged special collections and displays with related booklists in either libraries or in clubs. The Albemarle Report stressed the importance of co-operation between public libraries and the youth service, and recommended that libraries should remain open until 10 p.m. on some evenings in addition to undertaking the informal counselling of teenagers regarding vocational and recreational interests.

In 1954, 192 adolescent sections were maintained by 84 library authorities, but another 384 authorities made no separate provision. Preston was one of very few examples where a separate Youth Department was maintained, but many libraries considered that teenagers were not enthusiastic where these facilities were established.

A Library Service for Youth Sub-Committee was set up by the Library Association in 1961, and in 1963 a memorandum from the Executive to all branches requested the organization of regional conferences where necessary improvements could be discussed by lecturers, librarians, teachers and youth leaders. Conferences were held at various centres including Birmingham, Lincoln and Nottingham in 1963, and Lancaster in 1965. Leicestershire and Nottinghamshire county libraries were among the few authorities where serious work with teenagers was undertaken, although Islington and Staffordshire were responsible for well-produced booklists for the age group. A helpful booklist entitled *Attitudes and Adventure* was issued by the Library Association County Libraries Group in 1965.

Public-library–school co-operation was endorsed by the educationists in the School Library Association *School Libraries Today* (1950) and in the Newsom Report; and by librarians in the Memorandum of 1954 and the Working Party Report of 1962. Newsom pointed out that it was insufficient to restrict co-operation to the persuasion of pupils to acquire library tickets, and to the insertion of library periods into the school timetable. All avenues must be explored to ensure that children continue reading and using books after they have left school.

In 1954, 63 county, 43 county borough, and 46 smaller libraries received grants from the L.E.A.s for the supply of books to schools. Some libraries, however, did not receive grants, but still supplied books. Unfortunately 4 counties, 36 county boroughs, and 162 smaller libraries did not operate a service to schools. By 1962 most of the larger municipal and all of the counties in the Working Party survey provided books to schools on behalf of the L.E.A.s, but normally these collections augmented existing school libraries, and were often loaned for the purposes of book selection, as background material for teaching, or for special exhibitions. Many counties maintained exhibition collections including Derbyshire, Kent, Lancashire, Lindsey and Holland, and the West Riding, and there was a similar service in some boroughs.

Other services to schools included talks; instruction in the use of the public library to visiting parties; the provision of homework facilities; the loan of special materials for school projects, as at Buckinghamshire and Lindsey and Holland; special facilities for teachers; courses in school librarianship, as at Buckinghamshire and Staffordshire; and the provision of lists of books. In the latter category, outstanding publications were issued by Staffordshire (*The School Bookshelf*), West Riding (*The School Library*), and Wiltshire (*Prospector*).

The Library Association Staff memorandum of 1963 emphasized that the responsibility for fostering and maintaining the fullest co-operation was that of the children's librarian. In 1947, county library organizers of school libraries and work with young people were appointed at Hertfordshire, Lancashire, and Nottinghamshire, a development which was imitated in other areas. The joint School Library Association and Schools Section report of 1945 had recommended that these organizers should be appointed by the L.E.A.s and should be ex-teachers. The Library Association in its Memorandum of 1945, on the other hand, had advocated joint appointments of trained librarians by the public library authority and the L.E.A., although very few would hold qualifications in both librarianship and teaching. It remained the policy of the S.L.A. that school library organizers should have teaching and school library experience, an attitude which once more revealed a dichotomy of opinion between the two bodies.

Too often there has been conflict between librarians and teachers regarding the function of each, and none of the acrimony has served to benefit the children at all. For the future these problems will require settlement, and the individuals concerned will require a deeper degree of understanding the one for the other, or progress will be as unsatisfactory as it has so often been in the past.

CHAPTER 22

Literacy For All

IN THE course of this volume attention has been drawn to the changing definitions of literacy throughout the 19th and 20th centuries. The most expected of working class children by the Government at the time of the Education Act of 1870 was that they should be able to read a newspaper on leaving standard VI. An ability to enunciate words was regarded as sufficient even if their meaning was not understood, and many of the school books were so unrelated to the abilities and experiences of children that a lack of comprehension was commonplace. After 1870 a higher degree of attainment was necessary, and in the Code of 1881 intelligence and fluency in reading became requisite.

Accuracy, fluency and intelligence in reading are themselves insufficient but must be accompanied by an appreciation of what is read, an accomplishment which might take the form of enjoyment and/or inspiration. It is true that the reading of poetry was included in the requirements of the Revised Code of 1862, although the examples to be found in reading books were often open to severe criticism, but the opportunity for a development in taste was enhanced after 1870 with the introduction of English literature into the syllabus. This was taken a stage further in 1882 when the *Requirements in Reading* were extended to include passages from the works of Milton, Shakespeare, and other standard authors. This progress was of course related to the longer period for which children remained at school, and the index of backwardness was substantially diminished between 1872 and 1886. It must be regarded as essential that any subsequent raising of the school leaving age should be associated with a further broadly based rise in literacy.

The Cross Commission viewed the art of reading "as the key of all knowledge", which would open to the individual unlimited possibilities. Unfortunately this ideal did not reflect the rather unsatisfactory rate of progress in the schools, but the reality rendered the dream no less true. Throughout the 20th century it has been recognized that children should learn to read both for profit and for pleasure, and the principal reason for their failure to attain the second aim appears to stem from an inappropriate approach to the teaching of reading in schools.

Newsom has shown that literacy is not something which "is achieved once for all", but is a continuing process related to the abilities of the individual and the demands made of him by society. Crowther goes on to demonstrate the requirements made of meritocrats without which they will be either illiterate or innumerate. However, a survey of literacy in South London in 1966 revealed that 38% of the school leavers, and probably 20% at a national level, were incapable of reading a newspaper satisfactorily. The progress of a century appears extremely uncertain in the light of a revelation of this magnitude. There can be no room for congratulations in a system which expects its intellectual cream to be both literate and numerate whilst 20% of the total remains illiterate. It is economically feasible, surely, for all the children of this country to be educated according to their abilities, but in fact this is not taking place.

In 1961 the *United Kingdom Reading Association* was formed to encourage the study of reading problems, and this body promotes and stimulates research into the subject. At the inaugural meeting of the Hertfordshire branch of the U.K.R.A. in 1966, Dr. Joyce Morris stressed the need for better teacher training as the key to children's reading. She claimed that insufficient attention is given to the subject whereas it is important "to get reading recognized as the first art". It is imperative that the authors, illustrators, printers and publishers of reading books should be closely associated with the teachers in schools and colleges and those who undertake research into reading methods, so that the result of their liaison might be wholly beneficial to the children.

The Plowden Committee Report on *Children and their Primary Schools* (1967) agreed with the conclusions of the survey *Progress in Reading* (1966) which had been carried out on its behalf, that the standards of reading have risen steadily since the war, but the improvement has not been distributed evenly throughout the country. The problem goes far beyond teacher training and the quality of reading books and is closely related to deficiencies of a social character. The Plowden Report has emphasized the urgent need for more money, teachers, books and equipment to be channelled into schools in stipulated deprived areas where the school influence is counterbalanced by poor environments. Even if improvements in the majority of schools are to be delayed it is of primary importance that those in deprived areas should be raised to, and quite deliberately made better than the national average. A further demand of the Committee is that there should be expansion in nursery school provision, which, if realized, would ensure that an increased number of children would become acquainted with books at an earlier stage than hitherto.

When the mechanical difficulties of reading have been overcome the next step is to take full advantage of the newly discovered ability. There is a greater selection of outstanding literature for the profit or pleasure of children than ever before, and its availability to all is ensured, not only through the media of school and public libraries and in the form of prizes and gifts, but also by direct purchase. Increasingly, a variety of shops in the centres of large municipalities, in suburban areas and elsewhere, in addition to conventional booksellers, are displaying attractively coloured and designed paperback books which can be purchased for a few shillings. The vast increase in paperback publishing has provided the present generation of young people with unprecedented opportunities for the acquisition of personal collections.

There is still too large a proportion of the teaching profession which does not appear to be dedicated to the use of books with children. Many teachers lack interest in books, either due to a poor cultural background, or an absence of relevant courses during their period of training. It must be admitted that frequent "lip-service" is given to the advantages of books in education, but in numerous instances there is still a lack of understanding of what is required. In many areas there is a tradition of close co-operation between schools and public libraries, but in other instances the two organizations appear unable to work in harmony. Teachers and librarians must be condemned equally where they fail to co-operate with each other, and in their particular district are guilty of obstructing the road to literacy.

A ridiculous situation exists of public librarians censoring the very books which children appear to prefer. The majority of children are apparently indifferent to most of the books which have been awarded the Carnegie Medal. It is perhaps optimistic to trust that improvements in educational facilities and methods leading to a growth in literacy in the next few decades will serve to place good quality children's books in the most popular categories of reading matter. Improved as the publishing situation is, it is still true that an adequate availability of books for all ages, interests, and intelligences has not yet been achieved, but such a coverage must be regarded as essential to individual development. Once more there is an urgent need for closer co-operation between all who are concerned with the production and use of children's books, and this can be wholly satisfactory only if the children themselves are not excluded from participation in the discussions. In 1966 a Committee on Books for Children was formed which consists of representatives from the worlds of bookselling, publishing, education, and librarianship, but unfortunately the viewpoint of children is not directly represented. From the early days of writing for children, young people have been suspicious of literature which adults think they ought to read and no doubt they will continue to do so.

The Forster Education Act of 1870 was intended to ensure the provision of Elementary Education for All, and the Butler Education Act of 1944 sought to provide Secondary Education for All. The slogan for the 1970's and after could well be Literacy for All, although the exacting standards of the Crowther Committee will be required only of the minority. It may be appropriate once more to think in terms of children being able to read "a newspaper or other modern narrative" as a minimum rather than a maximum requisite of literacy, although one would hope that the selected newspaper would be chosen with care. There is too, a profusion of modern narratives which can be used as a basis for increasingly rewarding experiences in reading as an important factor in the education of the masters.

Select Bibliography

ADAMSON, JOHN. *The Illiterate Anglo-Saxon.* 1946. Cambridge U.P.

ALLEN, W. O. B. and McCLURE, E. *Two Hundred Years: the history of the S.P.C.K., 1698–1898.* 1898. S.P.C.K.

ALTICK, RICHARD D. *The English Common Reader: a social history of the mass reading public, 1800–1900.* 1957. Chicago U.P.

ARNOLD, MATTHEW. *Reports on Elementary Schools, 1852–1882.* 1889. Macmillan.

BARNARD, H. C. *A History of English Education from 1760.* 1961. London U.P.

BIRCHENOUGH, C. *History of Elementary Education in England and Wales from 1800.* 1914. University Tutorial Press.

BOOTH, CHARLES. *Labour and Life of the People.* 2 vols., 1891. Williams & Norgate.

BOOTLE PUBLIC LIBRARY. *Catalogue of Books for the Young.* 1891, 1893, 1896, 1901.

British Books in Print. 2 vols., 1965. Whitaker.

CLARKE, WILLIAM K. L. *A History of the S.P.C.K.* 1959. S.P.C.K.

COLE, G. D. H. *A Short History of the British Working-Class Movement, 1789–1947.* 1948. Allen & Unwin.

COMMITTEE OF COUNCIL ON EDUCATION. Minutes and Reports, 1839–1899.

CONFERENCE OF LIBRARIANS HELD IN LONDON. *Transactions and Proceedings.* 1877.

CREDLAND, W. R. *The Manchester Public Free Libraries.* 1899. Manchester Public Libraries.

CROUCH, MARCUS S. *Treasure Seekers and Borrowers: children's books in Britain, 1900–1960.* 1962. Library Association.

CURRIE, JAMES. *The Principles and Practice of Common-School Education.* 1862. James Gordon.

CURTIS, S. J. *History of Education in Great Britain.* 5th ed. 1963. University Tutorial Press.

CURWEN, HENRY. *A History of Booksellers: the old and the new.* 1873. Chatto & Windus.

DARTON, F. J. HARVEY. *Children's Books in England.* 2nd ed., 1958. Cambridge U.P.

EDUCATION, BOARD OF. *Consultative Committee on Books in Public Elementary Schools.* Report, 1928 (Hadow).

EDUCATION, BOARD OF. *Consultative Committee on Secondary Education.* Report, 1938 (Spens).

EDUCATION, BOARD OF. *Consultative Committee on the Education of the Adolescent.* Report, 1926 (Hadow).

EDUCATION, BOARD OF. *Consultative Committee on the Primary School.* Report, 1931 (Hadow).

EDUCATION, BOARD OF. Reports. 1899–1910.

EDUCATION, BOARD OF. *The Teaching of English in England.* Report, 1921 (Newbolt).

EDUCATION, MINISTRY OF. *15 to 18.* 2 vols., 1959/60 (Crowther).

EDUCATION, MINISTRY OF. *Half Our Future.* 1963 (Newsom).

EDUCATION, MINISTRY OF. *Primary Education: suggestions for the consideration of teachers . . .* 1959.

EDUCATION, MINISTRY OF. *Standards of Public Library Service in England and Wales: report of the working party.* 1962.

EDUCATION, MINISTRY OF. *Standards of Reading, 1948–1956.* 1957.

EDUCATION AND SCIENCE, DEPARTMENT OF. *Children and their Primary Schools.* 2 vols., 1967 (Plowden).

EDUCATION AND SCIENCE, DEPARTMENT OF. *Progress in Reading.* 1966.

EDUCATION DEPARTMENT. *Special Reports on Educational Subjects.* Vols. I and II, 1896–8.

EDWARDS, EDWARD. *Free Town Libraries: their formation, management, and history.* 1869. Trübner.

ELEMENTARY EDUCATION ACTS, ENGLAND AND WALES. *Minutes of Evidence, 1887.* Final Report, 1888 (Cross).

English Catalogue of Books, 1835–1965.

FIELD, MRS. E. M. *The Child and His Book: some accounts of the history and progress of children's literature in England.* 2nd ed., 1892. Wells Gardner, Darton.

Fifty Years: a brief history of the public library movement in Nottingham. 1918. Nottingham Public Library.

FITCH, JOSHUA. *Lectures on Teaching.* 1881. Cambridge U.P.

GREEN, ROGER LANCELYN. *Tellers of Tales: children's books and their authors from 1800 to 1964.* 1965. Edmund Ward.

GREENWOOD, THOMAS. *Public Libraries.* 3rd ed., 1890. 4th ed., 1894. Simpkin Marshall.

GREENWOOD, THOMAS, (Ed.). *Greenwood's Library Year Book, 1897.* 1897. Cassell.

GREENWOOD, THOMAS (Ed.). *Greenwood's Library Year Book, 1900–1901.* 1900. Scott, Greenwood.

GREENWOOD, THOMAS. *Sunday-School and Village Libraries.* 1892. James Clarke.

HAND, THOMAS W. *The Leeds Public Free Libraries.* 1903. Aberdeen U.P.

HEWITT, GORDON. *Let the People Read: a short history of the United Society for Christian Literature.* 1949. U.S.C.L.

HITCHMAN, FRANCIS. Penny fiction, *Quarterly Review,* 1890, p. 150.

Inquiry into the State of Popular Education in England. Report, 1861. Vols. I–IV. (Newcastle.)

JENKINSON, A. J. *What Do Boys and Girls Read?* 1940. Methuen.

Library, 1889–1898.

LIBRARY ASSOCIATION. *The Year's Work in Librarianship.* 1928–50. Library Association.

LIBRARY ASSOCIATION RECORD, 1899–1965.

LIBRARY CHRONICLE, 1884–1888.

LINES, KATHLEEN (Ed.). *Four to Fourteen: a library of books for children.* 2nd ed., 1956. Cambridge U.P.

MEIGS, CORNELIA (Ed.). *A Critical History of Children's Literature.* 1953. New York, Macmillan.

MORRIS, JOYCE M. *Reading in the Primary School: an investigation into standards of reading* . . . 1959. Newnes Educational.

MUIR, PERCY. *English Children's Books, 1600 to 1900.* 1954. Batsford.

MUNFORD, W. A. *Penny Rate: aspects of British public library history, 1850–1950.* 1951. Library Association.

OGLE, J. J. *The Free Library: its history and present condition.* 1897. George Allen.

SALMON, EDWARD. *Juvenile Literature As It Is.* 1888. H. J. Drane.

SALMON, EDWARD. What girls read, *Nineteenth Century,* 1886, p. 515.

SCHOOL LIBRARY ASSOCIATION. *School Libraries Today.* 3rd ed., 1961. School Library Association.

SECOND INTERNATIONAL LIBRARY CONFERENCE HELD IN LONDON. *Transactions and Proceedings,* 1897.

SELECT COMMITTEE ON PUBLIC LIBRARIES. Report, 1849.

SMITH, JANET ADAM. *Children's Illustrated Books.* 1948. Collins.

SMITH, W. H. and HARRAP, GEORGE G. *Survey of Boys' and Girls' Reading Habits.* 1957. Smith–Harrap.

SPALDING, THOMAS A. *The Work of the London School Board.* 1900. P. S. King.

TITMARSH, MICHAEL ANGELO. On some illustrated children's books, *Fraser's Magazine,* 1846, p. 495.

TUER, ANDREW. *Pages and Pictures From Forgotten Children's Books.* 1898/9. Leadenhall Press.

WOODWARD, E. L. *The Age of Reform, 1815–1870.* 1938. Oxford U.P.

YONGE, CHARLOTTE M. Children's literature of the last century, *Macmillan's Magazine,* 1869, pp. 229, 302, 449.

Index